CUSCO II
The Magic of The Munay-Ki
A Love Story

DIANE DUNN

CUSCO II
The Magic of The Munay-Ki
A Love Story

Cusco II

The Magic of the Munay-Ki: A Love Story

@ 2012 Diane Dunn

All rights reserved

CreateSpace

Charleston, South Carolina, USA

Cover and Book Design: Wendy Crumpler

ISBN: 1-4681-4475-8

For my dear husband Christer,
Thanks for inviting me into greater wholeness.

CONTENTS

PROLOGUE

Once upon a time there was a man and a woman who lived on Earth in different corners of the world. Before they came to Earth, they lived on the same star where they made a contract to meet when they knew the moment was right on Earth, to change the world.

Many years passed on earth and they experienced so much life they nearly forgot their promise. But one day, while the man and the woman were sleeping in their own corners of the world, the Star-Giver blessed them with a Star-kiss that helped them remember their soul contract.

In his dream the man saw a beacon of light from the high Andes Mountains in Peru. He packed his bags and journeyed to a small town along the river in the Sacred Valley not knowing the woman would be there. But because she too had been kissed by the Star-Giver, she remembered her promise and was awaiting his arrival. When they saw each other, their hands touched and their hearts remembered everything.

And so began their challenge to change the world.

The first world they needed to change was their own because they had become very set in their earthly ways, each having their own manner of managing their lives. His corner of the world was urban, neat and orderly. Her corner was mountainous, mystical and a bit chaotic. They had to adapt, release, heal and transform to see the other with eyes of love.

It was then the Star-Giver again came down from heaven and opened their hearts to envision a world where people lived in trust instead of the fear they had always known. The man and the woman were very happy their soul contract was now being fulfilled.

Together they learned to live with open hearts which made everything possible and all their dreams came true.

A few months after my first book was published, a woman calling herself Imaya, appeared at my retreat center in the Sacred Valley near Cusco, saying she had a message for me. She was sweet and disarming, but still I was a bit skeptical. She told me she was a channel. There was an entity she called Luz who wanted to speak with me.

During the first session we had together, Luz told me about a previous life in Atlantis where Imaya and I had been friends. I had been a young boy, privy to a special council that knew the "fall" was near. I was charged with taking the wisdom teachings of Atlantis to this region here in South America where I was now living.

In subsequent sessions I was given symbols by Luz and told to make specific ceremonies. We planted crystals on the property I own to activate certain energy ley lines. Luz told me the time was coming soon when a new phase of my work would begin but there were certain things I needed to do to prepare myself. By our last session together I was feeling overwhelmed by the energy and information I was receiving. I closed the door and Luz went silent.

Imaya herself seemed unphased by the information she was imparting as well as my reaction to it. She remained cheerful, warm and friendly throughout, even though I was sometimes rude and often suspicious. One day I was driving to Cusco with her when she said out of the blue, "Your man may be close at hand." I nearly slammed on the brakes. "What man!" I wanted to shout.

How could she have known that much of my journey from New York to Johannesburg to Peru included a longing to meet my soul mate? I had not discussed this subject with Luz. After moving to Peru several years before, I felt I had found my destiny and no longer needed a partner to feel fulfilled. My reaction to her statement – an odd mix of anger and fear – surprised me. I defensively told her I wasn't looking for a man. I was happy the way I was. She just smiled which irritated me even more.

My harsh reaction to her casual comment eventually led me to contemplate if in fact, I had really released my desire to find my soul mate. Perhaps reaching my fifties without committing myself to a long-term relationship was an indication that some growth and transformation was still needed. In my meditation time I sat down with Spirit to discuss what I could do. I said, "If I can heal whatever it is on my own, great. I will make that my intention and we can get started. If I need a relationship to do that work, then you deliver the appropriate man to my doorstep!"

And Spirit did.

CHAPTER ONE

GETTING HERE

The first time Peru came into my consciousness was in 1987 when I was living in New York City. I had recently closed down my theatre company and was looking for a new vocational direction. I went to see a psychic who said, "I see you in Peru." She may as well have told me she saw me on the moon. At that time, I wasn't remotely interested in Peru and politely told her she must be mistaken.

About that time I began meditating, conversing with God on a regular basis. This God I spoke with had a close resemblance to my Gramma who died when I was five. When she was alive, she showered me with such love and attention it was easy to imagine God was like her. This loving affirming Gramma God led me in surprising magical ways, first to Union Theological Seminary and a Masters in Divinity and then to South Africa just after the release of Nelson Mandela and the fall of apartheid in 1990.

I ran a church-based outreach program in Johannesburg for the homeless and unemployed of the inner city, which evolved over the years from feeding and comforting to empowering and healing – myself as well as the community. By the end of 1997 I was feeling it was time for me to move on, but I didn't know to where or with whom.

One night I read an article in the local newspaper about a visiting anthropologist named Alberto Villoldo who worked with spiritual healers in Peru. I decided to attend a talk he was giving and was riveted from the onset. Alberto spoke about his many trips from the United States to Peru, first for his PhD research and later for his own voyage of discovery, learning from an Andean master the ancient ways of healing by working with image and energy, beyond the western frameworks of time and space.

There were "channels of light" within the human body visible to certain shamans, he told us. The shamans were able to work with these channels, to see illness in people – physical, emotional, spiritual, which for them were all connected. They were also able to shift the energy within their patients in order to realign these rivers of light and restore health and well-being.

He told so many fantastic stories and even though I'd never heard anything like them before, a part of me was screaming inside, "YES, YES, YES, it's true. I know this is true and I want to learn how to it too. I want to meet these people." There was such a sense of urgency within me I'm sure I could have gotten on a plane right then. During the break in the 3-hour presentation, I went to speak with Alberto saying, "How can I go there and meet these shamans?"

He told me about a trip he was planning in June and promised to send information. Once again Peru had entered my consciousness, ten years after the psychic said she saw me there. Six months later I was in Peru. I knew even before I went, it would be an amazing opportunity that would change my life in a dramatic way.

During that first trip to Peru, I met two shamans named Regis and Sergio who would become my teachers. I invited them to come to Johannesburg to teach a workshop I would organize. That first workshop amazed me from start to finish. Everything fell into place perfectly although I didn't have the faintest idea what they needed in advance. I felt my consciousness expanding, although my mind couldn't comprehend it all in a logical way. It opened the door to my new life.

On their last night in Johannesburg, Regis shared with me a vision he had of a spiritual center in the Sacred Valley near Cusco. This was an ideal location because of its strong energy vortex, which would naturally attract people and assist in creating unity and transformation.

As soon as Regis spoke about it, I saw myself as part of this vision. In a moment of deep revelation, I knew I was moving to Peru. So by 2000 I was living in Cusco. Over the next seven years, that vision would become my own as I built and developed the Paz y Luz (Peace and Light) Center in Pisac, a small town beside the river in the Sacred Valley.

I first received the Munay-Ki Rites in June 2007 when some friends, teachers with the Four Winds Society in the United States came to stay at my Center. They had recently learned the Munay-Ki themselves and were excited to share with me the powerful love energy of this new form of initiation rites from the Andean Spiritual Tradition.

I didn't realize then how important these rites would become in my life and what amazing transformation they would bring me. A few days after Claudia first gave me the rites, I met Christer Lundin, the love of my life, who arrived on my doorstep just as I had requested from Spirit. A few weeks after that, I received my first invitation to teach the Munay-Ki to a group in Bariloche, Argentina. A few months after that, I completed my training with Regis and Sergio and began my own form of teaching the Andean Spiritual Tradition.

My new life with Christer and the magic of the Munay-Ki taught me what love really means. I invite you to let the magical Munay-Ki energy speak to you as you read these pages. Let it open your heart and your imagination to new possibilities.

CHAPTER TWO

MUNAY-KI RITES

The nine Munay-Ki Initiation Rites come from the Andean Spiritual Tradition in Peru.[1] The translation of *munay* in Quechua (the indigenous language of the Andes) is love. *Munay-Ki* means I love you. These rites became available to us in this form in 2007 after Alberto Villoldo as well as some Q'ero and other indigenous shamans with whom he works, were leading a sacred journey in the snow-capped mountains above Cusco in June 2006.

Alberto Villoldo, whom I first met at the talk in Johannesburg in 1998, is a Cuban-American psychologist and medical anthropologist who studied Peruvian shamanic healing practices in the '70s and '80s. He started the Four Winds Society in 1984 and has been teaching shamanic healing and leading groups to Peru for more than 30 years.

Alberto and the Q'ero shamans felt the time was right to share the energy of the traditional initiation rites in a form more accessible to people around the world.[2] They believe we are at a critical juncture in human history and sharing these Rites with as many people as possible will assist in the great transformation known as the *taripaypacha*, the time of meeting our true selves again.

Alberto says, "These prophecies of the ancient Americas speak about a new human appearing on the planet – one who lives free of fear and resides in his or her transcendent nature.

---

[1] There is a chapter on each rite but if you would like to see the full list with brief descriptions, see Appendix A

[2] There has been a lot of discussion about the origins and authenticity of the Munay-Ki. To read my thoughts and feelings on that subject see Appendix B.

The Munay-Ki Rites are the codes for the new human. They are delivered in the form of energetic transmissions and help us develop a new architecture in our luminous energy field."

These nine rites are given in this new form as the next step in the evolution of humanity, to realign and attune the neuro-pathways in the body and truly shift human consciousness. These Initiation Rites, in essence, empower us to step up to the task of being lightworkers for the Earth and all creation during this amazing time of transition.

The Munay-Ki Rites assist the recipient to heal the past and become a person of wisdom and power. As you experience these energy transmissions, you can feel the presence and sense the wisdom of luminous beings who have broken out of linear time and now dwell in sacred time. As you raise your level of vibration, these luminous beings will come to you and guide you.

The Nine Munay-Ki Rites are broken down into three categories: The Foundation Rites, The Lineage Rites and The Rites to Come. Traditionally, the Lineage Rites (initiations passed down from master to apprentice for many generations in the Andes) are given using a *mesa*, a medicine bundle with power stones from the sacred mountains. The Munay-Ki Rites are given instead with a donut shaped Pi stone.

The Pi Stone is symbolic of our luminous energy field, its circular shape representing the archetype for wholeness. The shape also represents the ouroborous, the serpent of light swallowing its own tail, constantly creating itself, and forming a circle. It symbolizes the eternal unity of things, the cycle of life, death and rebirth. The center represents our energetic spine, the kundalini energy that flows through the center of our bodies, symbolizing our own spiraling DNA. It is associated with the serpent of light coiled around the base of the spine approximately 3.142 times (π). When awakened, it spirals up your spine like a figure 8 around your seven chakras, creating a never-ending loop, opening you to higher consciousness.

When you have received all nine Rites and learned how to give them, you will be given a Pi stone. It is asked that you pass on the Rites to others. Once enough people have awakened to a higher level of consciousness, we will then witness the birth of a new form of human on the planet and the dawn of a new civilization, proving the adage, "We are the Ones we've been waiting for."

When I first received the rites from Claudia over a period of one week, I felt the energy increasing with each rite I received. By the time she gave me the last three rites, I felt a shiver pulsing through my body that surprised me. At that time what interested me most about the Munay-Ki was learning how to give the three traditional Lineage Rites which correspond to the initiations I had received from Regis and Sergio but had not learned how to give to others. If I was going to teach the Andean Tradition in my own way, I wanted to know how to initiate other people.

The Munay-Ki training would indeed teach me how to give the three Lineage Rites but I was reluctant at first to embrace all nine rites because I knew (as much as an outsider can know these things) that Alberto's way of teaching the tradition had different aspects to the way I had learned it.

Yet after learning the Munay-Ki, and even more so after teaching it to others, I realized that the energy of these Nine Rites is profound and powerful. The form and substance of the Rites had been codified by Alberto but the energy and purpose of the Munay-Ki is connected to an ancient tradition that reminds us of who we really are, beyond culture and country.

I watched my students transform in amazing ways in the short span of three days as they received the rites and learned to give them to others. Many of those students began to teach the rites themselves which changed their lives in even deeper ways. We live in a time when we each can learn from one another how to become our best selves. I teach the Munay-Ki because it empowers me and the ones to whom I teach it.

I delight in the circular feminine form in which the Rites are given and then shared, because the time of hierarchical control is over. What is special for me about the Nine Munay-Ki Rites is that anyone who wants them can receive them. After learning how to give them, you can share them with as many people as you'd like and teach others how to do the same. It is estimated that since the first Munay-Ki classes were given in 2007, more than 500,000 people around the world have received these rites. People are drawn to the Munay-Ki because they change lives in a positive way. There exists the trust and belief that through these rites we are connecting to a higher source to become co-creators of the world we are dreaming into being.

CHAPTER THREE

MAGIC

Magic is the extra ordinary. We call it magic because it is mysterious and inexplicable. It is actually an art. Magic is learning to tap into the unseen power of nature and the divine creation. The Andean Spiritual Tradition uses this art. When people from this region plant a kernel of corn, they trust Mother Nature will give 100 kernels back. This is the law of nature. It doesn't require intellect or science to teach that kernel how to multiply. There is something built into the kernel (and all seeds) that knows how to do that. Of course we have to fertilize the soil, make sure there is enough water, nurture and care for the sprout as it grows. But it is not of our doing that the kernel knows the "magic" of growing a stalk and ears of corn. This is innate to that kernel. This is the unseen power of nature and divine creation.

We of course, are part of creation and nature. We too have an innate ability to tap into that unseen power to create magic in our lives. Magic is called coincidence, serendipity, chance. Magic happens when we move beyond linear time and space so we can dream something into being. Yes, it requires attention, nurture and care to discover the language of that innate knowing within us and around us. But magic is all around us all the time, just waiting for us to notice.

The magic of the Munay-Ki is energy, a vibration with codes recognized by our innate wisdom which awakens something deep inside us, calling us to be ready for this big change that is coming. It is as if a part of us has lain dormant and, like Sleeping Beauty, these initiation rites wake us up to claim our destiny as light workers, healers, transformers – ordinary people who do extraordinary things.

This magic of the Andean Spiritual Tradition was already at work in my life even before I discovered the Munay-Ki, having received some of the rites in the traditional way while studying with my shamanic teachers, Regis and Sergio. Sometimes, however, I needed reminding to focus on the magic.

When I moved to Cusco in 2000, I wrote a book with my best friend Wendy Crumpler about all the magical experiences that had led me to Peru, and the teachings of the Andean Spiritual tradition. I organized workshops and initiations taught by Regis and Sergio. Unable to find a publisher for the book in the USA, we ended up self-publishing and selling it at the workshops in South Africa and Peru.

I thought when I moved to Cusco the book would be a vehicle for us to promote the vision of the spiritual center. I envisioned a popular best seller. I also thought a wealthy donor I knew would give us the money to buy land in the Sacred Valley for the Center. None of those things happened.

But many other magical things did.

After living in Cusco for two years, I decided to buy some land in the Sacred Valley and build myself a house. I chose Pisac because I liked the energy of the Inka temples there. Ruben, an aging farmer, agreed to sell me a small part of his farm close to the sacred river and I built my house of mud and wood, stone and glass. As these things go, it went over budget and by the time I moved in at the end of 2002, I was nearly out of money. So I decided to rent my small cottage and my two guest rooms to tourists to make some money. I put up a few signs and people started to come, lovely people interested in spiritual things.

I had bought enough land to build a small conference center but that would have to wait until I had more money. In March of 2003, during my morning meditation, I got a message. "Build the extra rooms first." The architectural plans included a building with four extra guest rooms to the side of the main conference area. Since this would be more affordable, I spoke to my parents about loaning me the money.

Two days later I was with a friend in her café in Pisac when a woman began talking with us and asked if there were any new hotels in Pisac. It turned out she was updating the Lonely Planet guide for Peru. I took her to see my house and told her I was planning to build some more rooms. She loved it and promised to include it in the guidebook. I had to make up a name on the spot. That's how Paz y Luz was born. By the time the Lonely Planet guide was released, the new rooms were ready. She wrote that Paz y Luz was a spiritual place run by a woman who does mystical tours. I couldn't have asked for better advertisement.

In 2005 Ruben sold the rest of his farm to other people who began building houses. As fate would have it, Joyce Canny, one of my new neighbors from Lima, read my book in English and felt compelled to translate it into Spanish. She and I became close friends as the project developed. We were planning to print and sell it to ourselves, like the English version, but one day while she was translating it, her daughter came to visit with some friends from Lima who worked for Planeta Publishing Group, the largest Spanish language publishers in the world.

After reading it, they agreed to publish the book but thought it needed more material. Joyce suggested I add questions and answers at the end of each chapter and give people practical exercises to do. Planeta was pleased with the new material and published the Spanish version in July 2006. Even though Planeta is a Spanish language publisher, they agreed to publish the English version as well because of the large number of foreign tourists visiting Peru every year. They titled the book, *Cusco: Gateway to Inner Wisdom.*

The book sold well in both languages and later was published in the USA. The first year I received over 200 letters from people in more than 45 countries, saying how the book touched them.

Through that book I have been invited to teach the Munay-Ki in Argentina, Holland, Denmark, Sweden, USA, Italy, Australia, Norway, South Africa, India, Serbia, Mexico, Hong Kong, Kuala Lumpur, and Thailand.

Indirectly through that book, I met Christer.

Magic happens in many ways and forms when we set our intentions clearly and then release them to the winds of spirit to manifest in ways we often least expect.

In 2006, just before the first book was published, my chiropractor friend Howard arrived in Pisac and announced we were starting the Paz y Luz Healing Center. I was resistant at first because I was focused on organizing the Interspiritual Gathering planned for early August that year. Having spent most of 2005 building more new guest rooms and a conference room plus getting the book ready for publication, I was still in my practical mode.

But thanks to Howard's gentle persistence, the Healing Center was born. Magically, as soon as we put up a flyer offering Andean energy healing, inner child meditations and Network chiropractic, clients started to come. I was graciously reminded my calling is to be a healer (not a builder or events organizer). I knew the building and organizing was significant but now that things were in place, it was time to reconnect with this important part of myself.

For many months prior to this, I was focusing a lot of attention on organizing our first Gathering to manifest Regis' vision of the Spiritual Center. I was frustrated because it wasn't going the way I had hoped. I was trying to get spiritual leaders and their followers to come together at a big hotel in Pisac. I envisioned more than 100 people. Six months before the event, there were only 20 people registered and none you might call "spiritual leaders". I could not find any magic as I continued to push for my original plan.

At that point, I presented my proposal for the Gathering to the Interspiritual Dialogue Group of which I was a member. One of the other members made a casual comment that he might like the Gathering better if it was without a leader or set program.

Though the remark was not a directive, it clicked with me. I had spent many hours in leaderless circles with both children and adults working through all kinds of issues. I knew the power of that non-hierarchical structure. I began to formulate a different plan. We would wait until everyone gathered to make decisions about what the program would be. I created an outline for the event and that loose structure would be our starting point. On day one, we would envision the world the way we wanted it to be. On day two, we would experience it. And on day three, we would manifest the world the way we wanted it to be.

In February, I went to Canada to visit my friend, Wendy. A production artist, she volunteered to design a logo for the Center and a new poster for the Gathering. As we created and refined the poster, the sense of the Gathering's significance began to shift. The more we talked, the more we felt the Gathering should happen, needed to happen, regardless of how many people were present.

We had both seen the film, *What the Bleep Do We Know!?* and decided to rent it for inspiration. The filmmakers of the movie started with an idea but no clear picture of where they were headed. Yet, through their willingness to march into the unknown they had created a worldwide sensation. We watched, becoming more and more excited. Suddenly it made perfect sense why we had no leaders signing up: each and every participant in our Gathering would be invited to become a leader, sharing with the group whatever talent, knowledge or ability they possessed.

Though I still was concerned only 20 people were signed up, Wendy assured me the people who came would be exactly the right people. "And, Diane," she told me, "Jesus started with only 12. I'm sure 20 will be plenty."

On my return to Peru, during a day-long retreat, I had a clear message: "The reason there are only 20 people is because it is important for you to hold the Gathering at Paz y Luz, to launch your new conference room and to launch your own work there."

Once I turned inward to my innate wisdom and began to trust the process, magic began to flow. When the day of the Gathering arrived we had 24 people from six countries and four continents.

Few of the 24 were what would traditionally be considered leaders but every one of them found a way to come into their own power and lead the group. Even a landscape architect from Australia and the owner of a nursery in Peru teamed up to teach a wonderful seminar about living in harmony with the plant kingdom. I had never experienced a spiritual group that was so much fun while still being deeply transformational.

We danced, we sang, we painted, did yoga, played a game, put on a play, played with clay and sat around a campfire sharing stories and songs from our native countries. It happened that six of the 24 were Reiki practitioners who together did a group Reiki session with the rest of the Gathering. We worked individually, in small groups and as a community.

Our three days together seemed to have passed in a flash and yet time was suspended and everything we envisioned seemed possible, even likely, because we had experienced it and knew it was real and worthwhile. We were now prepared to manifest the world the way we wanted it to be.

Our way to manifest would be a day-long "sand-painting", the art of magic. The 'canvas' was a plot of ground 30 meters square – a plowed corn field that was marked out in the shape of the Inka cross, called a chakana. It would soon be a labyrinth of flowers and alfalfa but now there was only a circle of river stones 6 meters (20 ft.) in diameter in the center of the field. We each collected stones and trinkets and other objects found in our rooms or on the property that would become the people and situations we chose to depict and transform.

The principle most important to the magic of a sand-painting is that by working with energy and intention we are able to empower each object not simply to represent the person or situation we want to change, but to actually become it. At the center of our dirt canvas, we placed a heart-shaped stone, to represent Source.

We began with a centering meditation, focusing on a situation in our personal or community life we wanted to change. Then we took a spot just inside the circumference of stones. We each created a collage of our situation as it currently existed. We went around the circle and shared what we created. Because of what we had been through together in the previous days, the level of trust and openness was palpable. We surprised ourselves by going deeper than we already had, our previously hidden dark sides coming into the light. Tears flowed as truths were revealed and doubts and worries exposed.

Perhaps before we arrived at the Gathering, we thought what prevented us from our vision of a peaceful world were the raging wars in the Middle East or the vanishing rain forests.

But now, inside our circle of stones and love and grace, we saw before us the wars within ourselves and our families. We saw our disconnection from Mother Earth and Source. The sharing of these truths was possible because of the ground work we laid in the previous days. The good news was we were about to change and transform these situations, not in far-away lands but right here and right now.

We were then invited to shift our sand-painting to make the situation what we wanted it to be. Sharing again around the circle you could feel the transformation that had occurred, see it on the smiling faces, hear it in the tenor of each voice.

At lunch we hummed with satisfaction for our sense of accomplishment. But our work had only just begun, for with each shift of the sand-painting comes a new situation. It was time to revisit our canvas, as a changed person and sense what else now needed to be addressed. To work with energy and intention requires a leap of faith, a willingness to operate beyond what the mind can hold. Therein lays the magic.

The next shift was somewhat disconcerting. What did this new situation require of me? How was I changed by the act of transforming life as I knew it before? What did I want to do now? This next shift was done on our own, without sharing. It was private internal work.

Just before sunset we shifted our sand-painting one last time, moving even closer to Source in the center of the circle. With everyone's permission we were encouraged to move not only our own objects but also one another's if we were so inspired. Blockages were discarded and all obstacles removed.

Tentative connections were made stronger and distances diminished. Love, hope and harmony prevailed and all was connected with Source.

As we shared our final piece of collective art, one at a time around the circle, we felt complete. We held hands and toned a sound that ebbed and flowed, high and low, harmonic and dissonant. We held the tone, the sound, the vibration for some time until the energy was strong enough to lift with our hands and send out into the universe with a shout of joy and hope.

As the sun set, we dismantled what we had created, saving the pieces we wanted and returning the rest to Mother Earth. We dismantled it because life is not static and what we manifested was now set in motion to unfold in its own way.

That magical Gathering made me realize my vision for the spiritual center was actually different than the vision Regis shared with me in Johannesburg in 1999. Regis saw buildings and land, leaders and organizations where I saw spirit orchestrating a symphony of serendipity; people coming together to sit in a circle sharing their visions, creating consensus.

I had a great deal of love and respect for Regis but I could see our paths were beginning to diverge. The Gathering was the launch of Paz y Luz as the Spiritual Center and my own work within it. It felt like some secret door had opened and I was tentatively walking a new path.

During the Gathering, I had a lucid dream where Regis and I were standing in a passageway in my house. He began to change shape into an extraterrestrial being. I had a moment of panic before I was sucked out of my body and into the ground like a fast roller coaster ride. Soon I was in another world where a guide was waiting for me and led me to a new archeological site. It felt like Peru but wasn't anything I recognized.

After the Gathering was over, I felt this new magical energy continue to pulse within me. Across the river from my house is a mountain with a rock formation that looks like a carved Inka wall. Each time I looked at it when I woke in the morning, I felt called to go up there. A few weeks later, for my birthday, I hiked up there with two friends with tents and camping gear. I had a very strong feeling there were extraterrestrial beings who planned to meet me there.

I was exhausted from the seven hour hike and as soon as the sun went down at 6 p.m., the temperature dropped dramatically since we were over 12,000 feet (4,100 m). My friends were sharing a tent and I had my own. I have difficulty sleeping at high altitude so I lay awake for several hours talking to Spirit and waiting for something to happen. About midnight, still wide awake, I felt a strong energy enter my tent and pull me out of my body in a white luminous whoosh through the right side of the tent. I'm not sure how long I was gone or where I went, but I felt my being return to my body, still awake in my sleeping bag.

My heart was pounding as I asked whoever it was, what they had done. The answer I received was, "Don't worry, we are just working with you." Five minutes later I was once again pulled out of my body, but this time through the left side of the tent. This time I was more relaxed and even excited by the journey and the sensation of this white light. The next thing I knew

I was back in my sleeping bag. The experience felt similar to the first time but also different, like one tone differs from another even though both are musical.

This happened two more times until I had been pulled out all four sides of the tent. I saw some symbols and always sensed this very clear white luminous light as I was being pulled out of my body. The messages were always reassuring but incomprehensible to my logical thinking mind. I knew I had been called up to that mountaintop precisely to connect with these beings but even now I still can't explain what really happened except to say it was magical.

A few weeks later, Imaya came to stay at Paz y Luz saying she had a message for me. When she channeled Luz, who had told me about my previous life in Atlantis, I was more skeptical than fascinated. My practical mind was approaching overload with all this "new" information and experiences, which could explain my defensive reaction when she told me my man was close at hand.

The Spanish version of my book had been released two months before and already I was receiving letters from readers and requests for interviews. The secret door that had opened onto my new path was exciting but also somewhat intimidating. With the ET camping experience still fresh in my mind, the messages from Imaya seemed overwhelming. I don't think I closed the door completely, but I definitely decided to take a little break.

Six months later in April 2007, I received a visit from Fernando, a Peruvian tour guide who had been living in Sweden for

20 years. He brought groups from Sweden to Peru three times a year. On his previous visit he bought and read my book in Spanish. He was very interested in my story, discovered I lived in Pisac and came to meet me. I suggested he bring his next group, scheduled for June, to Paz y Luz for one day and night so I could do a workshop with them on the four elements and the Andean tradition.

Christer was part of that June group, which turned out to be the last group Fernando brought to Peru. The magic continued to flow, with results that surprised even me.

CHAPTER FOUR

LOVE

I led Fernando's group in a one-day workshop on the Andean Spiritual Tradition. After the morning session, I went over to talk with Christer. Somehow our hands touched, each right on the other's left. There was a strong current pulsing through us in a rapid circular motion. We looked into each other's eyes saying nothing.

The workshop continued without any chance for us to process what happened until that evening when Christer approached me and asked, "What was that – the energy flowing through our hands this morning?" My heart started to pound as if it had just occurred to me that I was attracted to this tall gray-haired handsome Swede. "I don't know," I said, "but if you'd like to discuss it, come in."

We talked with each other like old friends. The strength of our energy connection was matched by the connection of our personal interests, spiritual journeys and mutual attraction. Christer was a business consultant from Stockholm who was on a spiritual search, he told me, open to changing his life.

I had never met a man with whom I was so instantly comfortable. It was as if we had known each other all our lives. The conversation flowed and soon I was snuggled up under his arm. It felt so natural. No fear, no doubt, just delight. Before we knew it, it was 5:30 a.m. and time to say goodbye as his group departed at 6 a.m. for their train to Machu Picchu. Two days later we met in Cusco and leaving the group, he spent the rest of his week with me. In September, I visited him in Stockholm for ten days. By the end of the year, he moved to Peru to start a new life with me.

The week before Christer and his group arrived, Claudia, Wake and Kinlen, who had studied with Alberto at The Four Winds Society, were staying at Paz y Luz and they told me about the Munay-Ki. Claudia gave me the Nine Rites without teaching them to me. I felt their energy pulsing in my body. Perhaps that was what enhanced the energy that flowed through our hands when Christer and I first touched. Maybe the Munay-Ki magic was already at work in my life.

Wake and Kinlen came back to Paz y Luz the week after Claudia. Wake had taught the first Munay-Ki courses offered by Four Winds. He told me more about the Munay-Ki. I was particularly interested in learning to give the Lineage Rites, which are the traditional initiation rites of the Andean Spiritual Tradition.

I had received those rites from my teachers, Regis and Sergio, who said that women could receive the rites but not give them to other people. This had never made sense to me. Wake told me both Don Francisco and his wife Juanita, a shamanic couple from the Q'eros, gave these rites. In fact, Juanita had learned the rites from her mother and grandmother. This confirmation that female Andean Shamans had been giving the rites for generations, made me confident it was time for me to learn how to give the rites as well.

Learning the Munay-Ki was the first step, so I could share the rites with others. I asked my friend Jamee, who taught classes at Four Winds, to teach the Munay-Ki at Paz y Luz. I also invited Francisco and Juanita to share some rites in the traditional way. So between my visit to Stockholm and Christer moving to Pisac, I learned how to give all nine Munay-Ki Rites.

About that time, I received a letter from Sylvia in Bariloche, Argentina. She had bought my book in the Lima airport passing through Peru on a trip from Venezuela. She invited me to Bariloche to teach a workshop on the Andean tradition. A few weeks after Christer moved to Peru we left on a holiday together which started in Bariloche. I intended to give a few of the rites during the two-day workshop but during our correspondence, Sylvia asked me if I would teach her and her friends all the Munay-Ki Rites. I agreed to add a third a day if she could get at least six people. There ended up being 27 people for the two-day workshop and 19 of them stayed to learn the Munay-Ki, 20 if you count Christer.

This is when I really began to feel the love frequency of the Munay-Ki in a whole different way. Giving the rites to that many people in a row, I would go into an altered state as the energy of the rites flowed through me into them. I could sometimes see past life connections with the recipient. Other times I would receive messages for them from Spirit. It was as if time/space barriers disappeared or were easily crossed.

When I learned the Rites from Jamee, I did not intend to teach them as the Munay-Ki. I just wanted to give the lineage rites and teach the Andean Tradition as it was taught to me. But the Munay-Ki energy was moving in me in such a way that more invitations to teach them continued to come, until the energy of the rites themselves made me see this was my calling, the new focus of my work.

Part of the Munay-Ki magic is also the opportunity to look at one's shadow side so it can be cleared and transformed. My relationship with Christer in our first months together offered many opportunities for me to look at my shadow. Christer and I got along amazingly well in Bariloche during the Munay-Ki workshop and afterwards with some good friends of mine in Buenos Aires. Christer was so adaptable and easily able to socialize with people he hardly knew.

When we flew up to Florida to visit my parents, Christer charmed them immediately as if he had always been part of the family. So when we got to St. Lucia, an island paradise in the Caribbean where we rented a small cottage for a month, I was shocked to encounter a whole new side of Christer. When it was just the two of us alone together all manner of old wounds were being triggered without us knowing quite what we were triggering in the other or how to handle the response.

One day we decided to rent a car and explore the island. Christer chose to drive even though I was more familiar with driving on the left side of the road. That made me the navigator. As we left the small port town where we picked up the rental, I told him to turn left while following the map on my lap. He asked me again if I was sure and I insisted I was correct, pointing to the map as evidence. When we hit a dead end in a road where it was difficult for him to turn the car around, I realized I had the map upside down.

He was clearly angry but chose to go inside of himself instead of expressing his feelings verbally. My favorite way of solving problems is to discuss and identify the feelings that were triggered as to better understand how to avoid the same situation in the future. So Christer's silent treatment both hurt and infuriated me. The worst part was I was stuck in the car with him for several hours with no relief from the tension I was feeling.

We eventually made it back to our end of the island and returned the car. It was February and near to Valentine's Day. As we wandered silently around the town, I went into a jewelry shop where I'd hoped Christer would get the idea to buy something for me to express his love. Instead, he went outside to wait for me. I reminded myself that I had called Christer into my life to heal my issues with love and commitment. I began to turn my focus from him and the "problem" to inside myself to locate the source of my own frustration.

I decided to buy myself the golden heart that I had hoped Christer would have chosen for me. I made a little pact with Spirit: if Christer noticed the heart I wore around my neck, it would be a good sign our relationship would work out. I wore it a few times without comment from Christer. Just as I was about to give up hope, we went on a sunset cruise for Valentine's Day. As the sun was setting, sipping our complimentary rum punches, he smiled that sweet smile of his, with a sparkle in his eye and said, "What a beautiful heart you're wearing. Is it new?" "Yes, my darling. It is a gift from you." As I smiled back at him,

I could feel my heart opening once again to the love flowing between us.

Back at Paz y Luz there were more adjustments to be made, to make *my* house *our* house. Christer too had his struggles being far from home in a land whose language he didn't speak, with no job, no friends, and none of his familiar comforts and customs. Things were not going as smoothly as we'd hoped.

In April 2008, when things were particularly tense between Christer and me, we hosted our second Gathering to Envision, Experience and Manifest the world the way we wanted it to be. Jamee, my Munay-Ki teacher and one of the participants, led us on a meditative journey to the Upper World, to envision the world the way we wanted it to be – first, on a personal level, then on a community level and finally our vision for the world.

The first part of my meditation was clear and immediate: It was important for me to be part of a loving couple, to allow Christer into my heart fully, without guarding or protecting myself. On a community level, I saw the safe haven I was creating at Paz y Luz, where people could come to learn, grow, heal, transform, discover their true selves, open their hearts, to live free from fear. This was my vision for the world as well – a place free from fear, where all people live with open hearts, able to express their hurts safely and gently in order to clear them and heal them, not inflict more on others.

Coming out of the meditation, we were each given a piece of clay and invited to intuitively express our visions with the clay. I first molded some of my clay into the top part of a man and a woman connected at the base as well as the arms,

U-shaped. Next I formed a flat container with small pieces of clay inside representing the people who come to Paz y Luz. Then I realized that the couple was part of the container so I attached them to the side. As I did so, I saw that the couple was also a model for the divine – male and female in perfect balance and union, watching over us all. The importance of me being part of a couple took on greater significance.

When everyone was finished, we came together in our circle to share our visions and clay pieces. Christer made a globe with an attached tower open at the top (like a vase), which he said was "United Vision", akin to the UN only better. He had a flower bud at the opening in the top with fully bloomed flowers around the globe. These represented projects inspired by the upper world, coming to fruition through United Vision. His second clay piece was a man whose head was removed and replaced by a flower. His head was held in his arms close to his heart. Christer said that was him sitting in his office in the tower of United Vision where he worked more from his heart than his head.

On the last day of the Gathering we did a dance/meditation called Sounding. The music was an epic story of a warrior who came home resolute to "fight no more" and discover how to live from the heart. As I danced I went into a deep meditative state. I received two very clear messages. The first was, "My gentle heart will fight no more." I realized in that moment that despite all my defenses, I do have a gentle heart and in order to live from it more fully, I need to let go of any form of fighting.

The second message was even clearer than the first, "You need to marry Christer."

Some people don't hear messages easily and others don't trust them when they do. But I have been receiving messages (mostly during meditations, ceremonies and healing sessions) for more than 20 years. I have gotten pretty good at deciphering what is my own mind-chatter and what is a spirit-given message. Both messages I received that morning were strong and clear and nothing my own mind had been considering.

Our next activity was both illuminating and affirming. Jamee led us in creating a sacred geometry mandala for manifesting our visions. The principle is simple: with intention and clarity, what we form in our mind, we begin to create in material reality – the art of magic. First in meditation and then on paper with markers and paint, we chose our symbol and invited Spirit to help us work to manifest our vision.

My symbol was two even-sided triangles connected with their points in the center. This hourglass symbol had been given to me in a meditation in 2001. I was told it was "heaven and earth". Inside the bottom triangle I put Paz y Luz, healing, conferences and the United Vision "Heartquarters". Below that triangle, I put a man and a woman with their outstretched arms touching – Female-Male Union.

On the right side of the double triangle symbol, I painted the Rainbow Bridge, connecting heaven and earth. On the left side, I painted a soft vibrant pink orange heart and wrote around it, "My gentle heart will fight no more." Where the two points of the triangles connected in the center, I wrote the word

"Trust". The tower of United Vision extended into the base of the upper triangle, with its flower bud falling down from heaven and blossoming below. In the "heaven" triangle I put my guides and spirit energy. Above that triangle at the top was another couple, arms connected, and I wrote Divine Feminine/Masculine Creator.

Jamee had laid out a few decks of cards used for guidance and divination. One deck had symbols with sayings. The one I picked said, "I choose to experience heaven on earth", which I wrote on the bottom of the paper. I was stunned at how perfect it was for what I had already drawn – earth reflecting heaven. Then I pulled an Avalon Wisdom card – Partnership! The card said, "Seek connection in all things. This is a coming together of ideas, the marriage between two people, the harmonious blending of energies. It's a portent of opportunity, where partnership exceeds the potential of the individual."

"Partnership exceeds the potential of the individual." This is why it was important for my work to be a couple, a partner with Christer. The vision and messages were coming together. The work of United Vision required both of us with all our differences and commonalities, Christer and me, female and male union. I was now understanding the connection between the personal and the collective in a more significant way. And the importance of making a commitment.

We were then invited to launch our visions through a story. Val, my storyteller friend, guided us in the creation of our once-upon-a-time story told from a future perspective about a time before the new world came into being and how it had happened. Mine went like this:

Once upon a time there was a man and a woman who lived on Earth in different corners of the world. Before they came to Earth, they lived on the same star where they made a contract to meet when they knew the moment was right on Earth to change the world.

Many years passed on Earth and they experienced so much life they nearly forgot their promise. But one day, while the man and the woman were sleeping in their own corners of the world, the Star-Giver blessed them with a Star-kiss that helped them remember their soul contract.

In his dream the man saw a beacon of light from the high Andes Mountains in Peru. He packed his bags and journeyed to a small town along the river in the Sacred Valley not knowing the woman would be there. But because she too had been kissed by the Star-Giver, she remembered her promise and was awaiting his arrival. When they saw each other, their hands touched and their hearts remembered everything.

And so began their challenge to change the world.

The first world they needed to change was their own because they had become very set in their earthly ways, each having their own manner of managing their lives. His corner of the world was urban, neat and orderly. Her corner was mountainous, mystical and a bit chaotic. They had to adapt, release, heal and transform in order to see the other with eyes of love.

Then they gathered together with friends who had traveled from near and far to help them envision a new world. They sat around the fire and dreamed their world into being by removing their heads and placing them on their hearts. It was then that the Star-Giver again came down from heaven and opened their hearts to envision a world where people lived in trust instead of the fear they had always known. The man and the woman were very happy that their soul contract was now being fulfilled.

Because the man and the woman had learned how to come together in the balanced union of Love and Light, they reflected the perfect union of male and female in the divine creator. They were able to experience heaven on earth and they lived happily ever after.

When the Gathering was over, I had quieted my logical practical mind enough to know from a very deep place within myself that I would marry Christer if he wanted to do so.

Before the workshop Christer went to Puno where he met a friend of mine who recommended he visit a psychic in Cusco named Elena. She doesn't speak English so he asked me to come along to translate for him. Christer was interested in finding out more about his spiritual path. Soon after the session began, Elena turned from Christer to me and said, "You two are thinking about getting married, aren't you?" I was a bit surprised because of everything that had happened for me during the workshop but I wasn't so sure Christer would have agreed with that statement.

She continued, "You should get married. It is important that you honor your commitment to each other in this way. You have a golden thread that is connecting your hearts. You would have met each other even if he lived in China. You have a destiny together. June would be a good month. I know it is soon but there is no reason for you to delay." Again I was surprised because soon after Christer and I met, I had a meditation where I saw us getting married in New York in June on my parents' 60th wedding anniversary. I knew Christer thought that was too soon so I was a bit embarrassed to translate what she said because I didn't want to put any pressure on him. He said he would think about it.

He was leaving for Sweden in two weeks and I would meet him there three weeks later, to teach the Munay-Ki and visit with his family. Then we would fly to New York together to celebrate my parent's 60th wedding anniversary at a weekend family reunion before returning to Peru.

While he was in Sweden before I arrived, he called me and said, "Let's get married in New York." He was ready. We both understood we had been brought together for an important purpose. Marriage would create the container that allowed our love to heal personal wounds. With this deep soul connection guiding us into partnership, we hoped the work of United Vision would blossom into its fullness.

We were married on June 26th, 2008, my parents' anniversary, just as I had seen it in my meditation. At the ceremony, Val told my Once-Upon-A- Time story. It was a magical day, celebrating love. It was also exactly one year since I first received the Munay-Ki Rites.

CHAPTER FIVE

EARTH

It is my belief the source of all healing comes from Divine Creator. As we open ourselves to that energy, healing, balance and transformation are possible. There are many ways to connect with the energy of Divine Creator but the one I have found to be the most simple and direct is by working with the four elements: Earth, Water, Air and Fire.

These elements are what connect us to nature and creation. We are them and they are us. By learning their ways, we tap into the laws of nature, the creative force, the art of magic. To know the elements in an intimate way, we can access the power of the *apus* (mountain spirits) and *Pachamama* (Mother Earth), and through them, the power of the Divine Creator.

When I teach the Munay-Ki Rites, I include practices with the four elements, even though they are not specifically connected with the Munay-Ki. I find the exercises we do with the elements help people to clear their own heavy energy and better process the energy of the Rites in order to tune in more deeply to their power.

The Earth element is the densest of all the elements and therefore the most accepting and forgiving. When we sit or lie on the ground, we can give all of our heavy energy to Pachamama. She receives and welcomes all of our "shit" like a gift, because for her it is fertilizer that enriches the soil and enables her to give us back new life.

This is one of the laws of nature. Everything has a purpose – a mutual exchange. There is a Quechua word *ayni*, which means reciprocity. As we give, we receive. As we receive we give.

We breathe in oxygen produced by trees and plants. They are sustained by carbon dioxide we exhale.

To Andeans, *Pachamama* is not simply the earth element. She is our living, breathing, life-giving mother who loves us unconditionally. We plant one kernel of corn and she gives back hundreds. We give her our heavy energy and she gives back new perspective and new life.

The Earth element cleanses and transforms. When we work with this element, we have the opportunity to tell *Pachamama* all our concerns, our hurts, our pains, our frustrations. Perhaps in our homes, we have a closet or a space under the bed, where we store all the things we no longer use but aren't quite ready to get rid of. When we work with the Earth, we get to clean out that closet residing within ourselves, where we have hidden away all the wounds of our past.

One exercise we use to cleanse and transform those wounds, is to lie on the ground on our bellies. We put our hands on top of each other forming a round hole with our thumbs touching. We then tell our loving mother everything, the whole story of who did what to us when. We tell her all the secrets hidden in our interior closets. We can feel free to cry or scream or just speak silently to our caring mother who receives all of our heaviness with love and understanding. For her it is a gift for which she is deeply grateful. When we finish, we then turn our ear to the ground and listen to what advice or message she has for us.

At first you may not hear anything but just like any relationship, as you develop it, she will begin to share more of herself with you. She will offer you advice and assistance. Messages come in many forms so open your heart and intuition and pay attention to sounds or songs or images that come to you. Trust that she is using the "fertilizer" you have given her to offer you growth and nourishment.

I met Karen from Denmark during a Munay-Ki workshop in Copenhagen in 2008. The venue happened to be very close to the place she grew up, where she had a very difficult childhood, especially with her mother. During the course, we worked with the Earth element, our sacred mother, to let go of what no longer served us. I encouraged people to both offer and receive forgiveness. Karen shared afterwards how the exercise with Pachamama triggered a fierce opening process for her, where difficult repressed issues from childhood came up to the surface again. She shared it was both magical and dramatically powerful. The healing process for her since then has been ongoing which she described in this way: "My life's puzzle is being brought back together again piece by piece through understanding and forgivingness. Thank you to Pachamama."

CHAPTER SIX

HEALER

the first rite

The first of the Munay-Ki Rites is called the Healer Rite. It connects you to a lineage of shamans from the past who come and assist you in your personal healing. These luminous beings work on you during your meditation and sleep time to heal the wounds of the past and of your ancestors. The energy of this rite also awakens your ability to assist others in their own healing.

Illness and well-being, in the Andean Tradition, are understood not only on a physical level but also on an emotional, psychological and spiritual level. There is no way to separate those parts of ourselves. We require healing when one or more of those levels are somehow out of balance.

When I practice Andean Energy Healing in private sessions with people, I work with the energy just above and around the body, to cleanse and balance the energy of all the layers. As I pass my hands over the physical body, I can sense where there are blocks in the energy field. Sometimes I receive messages about the root causes of those blocks, which I share with the patient at the end of the session.

This offers the patient an opportunity to do the necessary adjustments that will assist in his or her own healing process. I can release the block and restore balance but if the root causes of one's "illness" continue to operate in the behavior patterns of the patient, the same problems could reoccur.

The Healer Rite assists you with shifting these old behavior patterns that in some cases you have inherited from your parents and grandparents. The Healer Rite is transmitted into your cupped hands. It is a feminine energy connected with the love of Pachamama. This rite is given into the hands because it is primarily with our hands that we work, that we touch ourselves and others. It is with that tender touch that we heal.

A crucial ingredient for healing is forgiveness. When I was first learning the Andean tradition, I had a dream where there was a major dispute going on that I was trying to mediate. My higher self in the dream realized the only hope for change in the world was to rise above logic and fairness and allow universal love to take over; that we needed to let go of the injury, no matter how terrible. In the dream, I no longer felt the need to make the person wrong or hate them for what they did but rather to recognize "the way it is" and let it go with love.

When we become more unconditionally loving of ourselves, then we can also be that way with others, without having to make them wrong. This is the work of the Healer. As we appreciate what *is* rather than be upset by what *isn't*, life becomes so much easier. Then we can recognize the gift in everything as it is unfolding. There is so much love and joy to be had if we open ourselves to it.

In my dream I had a profound understanding of the importance of forgiveness, and acceptance. When you can forgive an injury someone has done, you are able to recognize your own humanity as well as the humanity of the other. It sets you both free to accept each other and yourself, to recognize you both are human beings who make mistakes.

Forgiveness allows healing and transformation to occur. It melts the barriers that divide and isolate you from others and from the divine. If you are angry or bitter or frustrated, your awareness of the other and of the divine is blocked from reach. You become diminished. You become closed and your life force drains away.

When you can forgive and accept that the circumstances are as they are, it frees you to become your best self. In the moment of forgiveness you are flooded with grace and many more possibilities exist than when your heart is closed and protected. Forgiveness defies logic. It doesn't make sense that you should let go of some horrible thing someone has done. Your logical mind tells you it is wrong. Bad things must be punished. But the truth is punishment only perpetuates people's pain. Forgiveness frees both the forgiver and the forgiven.

The Truth and Reconciliation Commission was established in South Africa after Nelson Mandela became president. It was one of the most powerful healing acts the new government set in motion. They decided not to punish people who had committed political crimes during the apartheid years. If people came forward and told the truth about their atrocities, they would be given immunity. Victims could testify as well as perpetrators.

I witnessed the mother of a slain black youth testify. She cried out to know the location of the bones of her missing son. A former member of the secret police came forward with tears in his eyes and explained to the mother and others how he and his colleagues had beaten the boy and thrown the body in a shallow grave. He explained where the body was buried. He broke down and wept, begging the mother's forgiveness. She embraced him, also in tears and thanked him for telling her the truth. This is one of many moving stories of unbelievable acts of forgiveness and healing, which helped to heal the soul of a nation. Every time I think there is something I can't forgive, I remember that mother.

Forgiveness and acceptance are truly our only hope for real healing and transformation. They require of us a broad vision – letting go of our limited notions of right and wrong, good and evil. They require instead a deep compassionate understanding of the nature of human beings. Love alone heals. Through forgiveness and acceptance our capacity to love and be loved expands. The Healer Rite assists us in doing that.

When I stopped working with Regis and Sergio in August of 2007, I wasn't sure what new form my work with the Andean Tradition would take. After nine years of study and practice, organizing and assisting with many workshops and initiations, I had asked them to consider treating me more as a colleague and allow me to help give the initiations. I was hurt by their refusal and saddened they appeared unwilling to adapt their method of teaching to work with me differently. I had learned a great deal from them and was very grateful for their wisdom and teachings, but I felt it was time for us to part ways.

As I practiced forgiveness, I began to see the opportunity I had to find my own way to share the teachings that had been so helpful in transforming my life.

When Sylvia invited Christer and me to Bariloche, I had the chance, not only to test my wings but to heal the hurt caused by the separation. Sylvia had assembled 27 participants in the beautiful lake-side venue in the western mountains of Argentina that form the border with Chile. It was an ideal spot for working with the elements.

We lay down on the grass outside our conference room to let Pachamama cleanse and transform all our heavy energies. I was delighted with the opportunity to clean away any heaviness from the past and to feel the embrace and support from our loving mother; to forgive and be forgiven. We did another exercise in the woods above the lake where we each picked a tree, putting our arms around it and our bellies against its trunk, feeling the roots beneath us and the branches reaching up into the sky.

When we came back to the conference room I felt confident, the sadness transformed into gratitude. I was excited to be sharing the Healer Rite in conjunction with our work with the element Earth. As the energy of those luminous beings flowed through me while I transmitted the rites to one person, then the next, I was surprised by the force of it. I could sense the pain of some of the participants as I connected with them before giving the rite. The more times I gave the rite the clearer my vision became. I not only perceived flashes of information but I could also sense emotions and situations. I felt I was channeling the energy of these ancestral healers, seeing and sensing through their eyes. I was beginning to glimpse the magic of the Munay-Ki. And it was wonderful to be sharing it with Christer.

It was the first of many times I experienced Christer's ability and willingness to support me as a teacher, without feeling the need to call attention to himself. He was present and available as an able assistant; completely comfortable with me leading. His personality was confident, warm and generous. The group loved him even though he hardly spoke a word of Spanish. His charm shone through beyond language.

When I first learned the Munay-Ki, my intention was to use the rites in conjunction with my other training in the Andean Tradition. I wanted to teach the tradition in a different way than my teachers had taught it to me. The form in which they taught the tradition was hierarchical; we had to master one level, before proceeding to the next. There were six vertical steps in all. This method is quite similar to most modern educational institutions. From what I knew of the indigenous shamans in the region, their apprenticeships with their teachers operated in a more lived-in organic way, over many years, not climbing a ladder.

As urbanized foreigners, who meet once a year with our teachers, we could not learn in the same way as the indigenous masters. Our teachers created a bridge for us between those worlds, which I appreciated. But their form did not always resonate with me. Their style of teaching was similarly hierarchical, with the "master" dispensing information to the student, while standing in front of the class.

I longed for another form and style for teaching this ancient tradition. It is my belief that an exchange of information can be mutually beneficial between student and teacher. Of course it is true that the teacher may have more information about certain things than the student but we all have something valuable to share. The give and take among participants is an important part of the learning process. This relates to the principle of anyi – as you give, you receive and as you receive, you give. The interchange is crucial.

Instead of standing in the front of the room, I prefer to set chairs in a circle, where we all sit together. I liked the Munay-Ki model which gives and teaches all nine rites together. Once you receive each rite, you learn how to give it, and then practice sharing the rites with each other. The exercises with the four elements seemed to work well interspersed with the rites. Since I was based in Peru and knew indigenous shamans, I thought it would be helpful to have them with us to do ceremony and share the lineage rites in the traditional way, while visiting sacred initiation sites in the area.

August first is said to be Pachamama's birthday. Eight is the Pachamama number and the entire month of August is said to be her month. Here in Cusco's Sacred Valley, the fields are prepared for planting in August and many offerings are made to Pachamama, trusting that she will give back a plentiful crop. So after Bariloche, I decided to lead my first 8-day workshop in Peru starting on August 1, 2008, combining the Munay-Ki, the four elements and the sacred sites together. I called this workshop The Full Circle.

My experiences in Bariloche teaching the shorter Munay-Ki course, confirmed for me that I was finding my own way that resonated deep inside my heart. I was grateful to my teachers for all they had taught me and for setting me free to develop my own style and form. The Munay-Ki Rites presented themselves to me at just the right moment, as part of the magic I was experiencing.

CHAPTER SEVEN

DAYKEEPER

the fifth rite

The Daykeepers were the masters of the ancient stone altars found in sacred places throughout the world, from Stonehenge to Machu Picchu. The Daykeeper is able to call on the power of these ancient altars to heal and bring balance to the world. The Daykeeper Rite is an energetic transmission that connects you to a lineage of shamans from the past.

According to lore, the Daykeepers call on the sun to rise each morning and set each evening. They made sure humans were in harmony with Mother Earth and honored the ways of the feminine. The Daykeepers were the midwives who attended births and deaths, as well as being herbalists, and traditional healers. They were generally women, and were knowledgeable about the ways of the feminine earth.

The Daykeeper Rite in the Munay-Ki, begins the process of healing your inner feminine, and helps you to step beyond fear to practice peace. The Daykeeper Rite is the fifth Munay-Ki Rite and the first of the three Lineage Rites. I teach this rite in conjunction with the exercises with the Earth element, which is why I place it here.

In the Andean Tradition, the energetic equivalent of this rite is the *Pampamisayoq* Rite. Pampamisayoqs, like Daykeepers around the world, work with Pachamama, healing and caring for the needs of their community. They know a great deal about the healing properties of the plants and herbs. They work in balance with nature.

Among the indigenous shamans in the Andes, the Pampamisayoq Rite is transmitted the traditional way using one's mesa. As shamans transmit this rite they call out loud the lineage of Pampamisayoqs, transferring the energy of this rite, through their mesa into the body of the recipient.

In the Munay-Ki, the Daykeeper Rite calls on this same lineage and transfers the energy into the recipient using the Pi stone. There are four main energy "gateways" in our physical bodies: the belly, the heart center, the third eye and the crown. The energy is passed by blowing into the crown and touching the other gateways with the Pi stone, then finally passing the energy from forehead to forehead.

The belly, heart center and third eye are three energy doorways that are related to the ancient Andean principles of life: *llankay*, meaning work or service; *munay*, meaning love and compassion; *yachay*, meaning wisdom. Many of the Rites transmit the energy through these energetic centers.

My first invitation to teach the Rites in Bariloche was followed by another opportunity to teach them at a friend's spiritual center in Sweden. Both these workshops inspired me as I prepared to offer the first Full Circle Initiation in Pisac in August 2008.

The Full Circle lived up to its name in ways I couldn't have guessed when I was first exploring my own way to teach the Andean Spiritual Tradition. We were full in numbers, full in diversity and full in activities.

Thirty-two participants from 21 different countries around the globe, sat in a circle in our round, glass conference room on August 1st. We called the names of ancestors along with our own, as we set the altar with our special objects from home and voiced our intentions. We gathered from North and South America, eastern, western and northern Europe, the Middle East and South Africa – from countries like Paraguay, Iran, Serbia, Lebanon, Palestine, Norway, Chile and Ireland.

Our diversity was expansive in other ways as well, with the youngest participant being 12, accompanying her mother for a special coming-of-age experience. Several women were in their 60s and all the other decades in between were amply represented. We had seven men and three couples. There were gay, lesbian, straight, black, white, Latin, Jewish, Arab, Christian and Indigenous. We were a beautiful rainbow of variety yet together we beat as one pulsing heartbeat, in tune with the mountains surrounding us. It was a full and auspicious gathering.

During our eight days together we worked with the four elements: Earth, Water, Air and Fire. We received the Munay-Ki initiations every day and learned how to share them. The first day with each element, we were based in Pisac at Paz y Luz. The second day with each element, we went to a sacred Inka initiation site unknown to most tourists. There indigenous shamans gave us the lineage rites in the traditional way to integrate with the energy of the place. Afterwards we practiced giving that rite to each other in the Munay-Ki form.

The first day, after our opening ceremony, Juanita and Francisco performed a *despacho* – a ritual offering for Pachamama, which we buried at sunset. We talked about the Earth element's cleansing power and lay on our bellies outside to give all our heavy energy to Pachamama. Later we received the Healer Rite, which we then shared around the circle with each other.

The second day, we went to a special womb-like cave to continue our connection with the Earth. After emerging, we received the Pampa Misayoq Rite (feminine earth energy) from Francisco and Juanita in a breathtaking spot looking down on Cusco. Then we shared the Daykeeper with each other, activating the healing process of our own inner feminine.

We worked with the other elements and shared the rites in two more special sites. Each day the experiences brought us deeper and deeper into ourselves, awakening new possibilities. For me, there were so many new opportunities. Even though Christer was in Sweden during this time, visiting his family, I felt his presence and support on this new journey of discovery.

Christer and the Munay-Ki had appeared in my life at just the right moment, as my work with Regis and Sergio was ending. One door closes and two more open.

CHAPTER EIGHT

WATER

The Water, our next element, washes and balances us. Water is the ruler of our emotions. Planet earth is more than 70% water and so are we. For this reason, according to my teacher Regis, our extraterrestrial brothers and sisters like to call us human beings "intelligent bags of water". Like the blood in our veins, the earth's water nourishes all her inhabitants. The currents and rhythms of water pulse through our bodies and enable us to feel connected with everyone and everything. Our body chemistry is an inextricable link to the planet herself.

The waters of this planet are ruled by the moon, which also has a significant effect on our emotions. Emotions make us human but we need to make sure we don't let our emotions rule our behavior. Water can teach us balance and adaptability. If a flowing river encounters a rock or other obstacle, it easily finds another route – over, under or around.

Water is a solvent, a cleaning agent in the material world. So it is in the spiritual world as well. When we engage with water, staring at a river or the ocean, swimming peacefully in a pool, we are being cleansed. All our sadness, anger, hostility, stress can dissolve away in the water.

When working with the elements, it is important to be conscious and fully present with your intention to connect. Take at least twenty minutes with no other task than to watch the water and breathe. You may, at first, run through the litany of things to be done, but if you stay and gently, gently turn your focus to the water, all of those things will float away in the water's current. You will be left with a peacefulness that enables you to be present to your life in a new way, not merely running through it, checking off tasks on your list.

When you can't get to the ocean or a river, there is a wonderful exercise you can do in the shower. The point is to release heaviness and let the water move it away from you. In the shower, allow the water to wash over you and become aware you are cleansing your energy field, not just your body. Let all your tensions, frustrations, and worries dissolve and melt down the drain. If you have taken on the heavy emotions of others, wash them away as well. Be conscious of the water, the way it looks, feels, smells. Thank the water for helping you in this way.

When you step out of the shower, you are clean and your energy field is clean. This means you are also vulnerable, so you want to seal your energy field to give yourself some protection from heavy energies that bombard you through the day. First, affirm who you are, the fabulous you that you know exists, then repeat three times. "I know who I am. Nothing and no one can change this." As you repeat these words imagine the light of Divine Love putting protection around you, a golden shield or bubble that radiates love and reflects love back to people even if what they send your way is heavy energy.

Water works in conjunction with silence to slow us down. You know this if you've ever snorkeled or been scuba diving. Surrounded by form-fitting liquid you float in a world moving in slow motion, you hear your breath and the beat of your heart. You slow down to match your surroundings.

This is also one of the properties of water. It takes on the shape of its container. Imagine the water in a raging river. Put that water in a glass and it becomes still and level. Tip the glass at an angle and the water again finds horizontal. Move it to a different container, the same thing happens. Put it back in the river and it picks up the current, moving just as fast as the water around it. No matter where it goes, it adapts and is always seeking balance.

Learning from the water, we too can adapt to all situations and stay balanced. We unblock our energy channels, which allows us to tune in to higher frequencies. Amerissis, a German friend who lived many years in Alaska before moving to Peru, had a beautiful experience with Water during a recent workshop with the four elements. This was a special group with people from Denmark, South Africa and Argentina, who had all received the Munay-Ki Rites in their own countries and were now here in Peru to deepen that experience. This is her story:

> The day of our work with Water, we were at a sacred site high above Cusco. We were led to an area away from the beautiful stream where Diane and the shamans were preparing for the water ceremony. We were instructed to meditate until we were called.
>
> I sat with my back against a rock and began to breathe deeply, listening to the enchanting sound of water flowing over the rocks below me. It was not long before I noticed an odd sensation down my spine and the sides of my body began to move fluidly as if by their own volition. There was a great joy in my body as I realized I was shape-shifting into a dolphin. At one point I even brought my hands to my face to feel my dolphin nose, the sensation of it was so strong.
>
> Three years earlier in Honduras I had the amazing

experience with eight others, of actually swimming with a pod of wild dolphins in the open ocean. I now felt my body calling me back into that joy, that freedom. It was exhilarating. I felt like I was returning home.

I had a dream 18 months before the workshop where I was swimming with the dolphins. I had all the attributes of the dolphins but I was in my human form. When I joined them the dolphins were so happy to see me. "Where have you been?" they asked. We played together for a long while but eventually my pod had to leave, and it was with great sadness I realized I could not go with them.

Sitting there on the mountain meditating, I felt connected with this group of people from three countries as if they were my pod. We had shared so much already and there was so much love between us. Yet I knew this pod at some point would also have to leave me as well.

"When," I asked the Water, "will I be able to always feel this kind of love and joy in my human body toward all of life?" The Water replied, "You're almost there." I was reassured the communal love I felt in my dolphin form would be experienced consistently by me one day soon.

Working with the Water, we learn to live life more calmly and more connected. As we release our heavy emotions, we begin to ask what is right for us in the moment and live more fully in the present.

CHAPTER NINE

BANDS OF POWER

the second rite

The second Munay-Ki Rite is called the Bands of Power. It is one of the four foundation rites. In the Munay-Ki this rite is given with the Pi stone. This is a very old rite in the Andean Tradition which was given with five special stones that had points on them. These stones were usually gifted from master to student.

The bands themselves are part of our energy body. They roughly correspond to the seven chakras in the eastern tradition, running from the crown to the base of the spine. These five energetic bands also represent the earth, water, fire, air and pure light. These bands are activated in your luminous energy field, and act as filters, breaking down into one of the five elements any heavy energy that comes your way so that these energies can feed you instead of making you toxic or ill. Once activated, the Bands of Power are always 'on'. In a world filled with fear and anger, the bands provide powerful protection.

The first band to be activated at the base of the torso is black in color. It connects the initiate to Pachamama and the power of the element Earth which will break down any heavy energy into fertilizer for Mother Earth.

The top of the next band is the upper part of the belly. This band is red in color and connected with the element Water. This band includes the solar plexus, the area of our emotions. The recipient is connected with the blood red power of water, *Mama Una*, in Quechua, which will breakdown any heavy energy encountered in this emotional zone and return it to the flow.

The top of the third band is the heart center. The color of this band is gold, connected with the power of the element

Fire, *Nina* and the golden sun which will burn away any heavy energy in the heart center and transmute it into love, passion and compassion.

The next band is silver, with the top border at the throat. This is the area of communication connected with the Air element, *Wyra*, which will blow away any heavy energy and break it down into a purified form.

The fifth band is the whole head and is pure white light. By activating this area the recipient connects with the power of the stars, constellations, moon, and Divine Creator which will transform the heavy energy into light.

I learned this rite in the traditional way (with the five pointed stones) from my teachers after five years of study with them. In the past this rite had an air of mystery about it. It was given with the eyes of the recipient closed, without explanation, so its form would remain secret. Its power was energetic, not logical or explainable.

In the modern urban world, we can feel pulled between the known world of material reality and the Andean spiritual model. We tend to trust our thinking analytical mind and practical experience in the everyday world more than the unseen energy of this tradition.

The Andean Tradition encompasses the dualities of life, both the light and dark. But we always have the option to choose which side we wish to engage with and focus on. We cannot always choose the circumstances of life we find ourselves in, but we can always choose how we will respond to those circumstances.

Most of the time those choices can be much simpler than we make them. It is usually our emotional reaction to circumstances that makes the situation feel difficult, more than the situation itself. Emotions can be shifted and released with the help of the elements which is why I teach the Munay-Ki in conjunction with these practices.

In order to embrace the essence of the Andean Tradition, you can connect on an energy level with the elements, nature and divine creation. You can trust this energy flow is guiding you and taking you where you want to go. That requires letting go of the need to know and understand things in a logical analytical way.

This can create some stress since most of us have been taught well how to analyze and understand everything as a way of controlling our reality. It feels much safer to most of us than the spiritual path, since it is so familiar. But that doesn't mean it works, just because it is familiar. This way of "controlling" things is just an illusion.

Sometimes on our spiritual journey we are pulled between these two modalities. To choose between the familiar and the unknown can be stressful, especially when we stand somewhere in between the old and the new rather than letting go of the old and choosing the new. We are neither in one place nor the other.

It is not possible to be in both at the same time because they contradict each other. The anxiety we sometimes feel has to do with emotions related to letting go of the old before we fully trust the new.

I had called Christer into my life in order to heal my issues with commitment and trust. But it still surprised me during our first year after getting married how many times we would both get stuck in our old patterns. For me, it was often when I was stressed about "practical" things at Paz y Luz.

In April 2009, Christer and I were offering a workshop called "Releasing Fear". The theme was Christer's idea as a follow-up to the Gathering in 2008 where he first conceived of United Vision. We had the workshop title and a few participants signed up but we hadn't discussed details for the program, which we intended to leave loose, allowing the participants to contribute their ideas as we went along.

Several people who had signed up backed out at the last minute but we had decided to go ahead anyway. A few hours before the workshop started, I sat down with Christer to discuss the format. We both pushed each other's buttons and closed our hearts to one other. In retrospect, the theme of the workshop should have given us a clue as to what was going on. Old fears that needed releasing had come out front and center.

But in that state of "shut down" it is hard to see even what is right in front of you. A wonderful teacher/healer was staying with us at that time. In my troubled state, I knew enough to realize we needed some help. I asked Akiyah if he would help us. The three of us sat in our conference room for almost two hours, lovingly guided by Akiyah, but it seemed for every step forward we took two steps back.

I thought I was really extending myself, giving my best to resolve the problem only to be hurt when Christer didn't respond the way I wanted him to. The workshop was about to start and I couldn't communicate with him, so how were we going to teach together? "Impossible", I said, which is exactly how it seemed to me.

Akiyah then suggested we "bracket" the disagreement issues and just try to remember that we loved each other. "Let go of everything but that", he said "and just feel the love I know you have for one another." The three of us held hands, closed our eyes and began to meditate. After some time, Akiyah left us holding only each other's hands. I tried to feel the love but I couldn't! I was trapped inside my own hurt and judgment, with no way out that I could see.

Then, Christer's energy shifted. He reached out to me, with love sparkling in his eyes and kissed me. In that instant everything changed, the gate to my heart swung open and the drama of the previous hours dissolved, vanished without a trace. There was only love – pure sweet love.

It is a sense memory I will never forget. In that instant I knew nothing else matters more than love. To feel love – your own for someone else or theirs for you – requires an open heart. When our hearts are open, everything is possible. When they are closed, we are stuck in a dark and dismal place. What astonished me was that problems can be solved without changing anyone or anything – except of course, ourselves. And the only thing we actually *can* change is ourselves!

What freedom there is in that truth. We think all our protections are necessary to keep us safe, but the best protection we can have is an open heart. I'd like to say I have never shut my heart again but alas, it isn't so. What I can say is more often than not, I look within when I feel closed-hearted rather than seek to change the other.

I believe there is something deep within us all calling us to learn this "new" way of being which is actually very old: the way of mystery and wonder and magic. Every minute of every day we get to choose how we want to respond to the circumstances of our lives, no matter what those circumstances might be.

Jacqueline, from England, who teaches the Munay-Ki, had this experience after receiving the Bands of Power for the first time:

> *I saw myself with inner vision going through the world and life so protected: As I walked along, someone sneezed towards me, the sneeze hit the fire band and was instantly transmuted; pollutants surrounded me yet they couldn't penetrate as the earth band took them and they became fertilizer in the earth; germs headed my way but the air band effortlessly blew them away. Someone sent envious/ negative emotions towards me but the water band simply dissolved them- washing them away, and disasters occurred in the world but the pure spirit band of light stopped me from going on a plane that might have a problem or to places where a natural disaster was imminent, etc. I felt so incredibly safe and grateful! (As you may know I'm always travelling and leading adventurous expeditions or yoga retreats in remote places so that was super reassuring!)*

When we work with the elements, talking to Pachamama or spending time with the Water at the sea or the river, letting it soothe and smooth us, they help us to release our emotions, our fear, worry and stress. This allows the heart to open and love to flow.

Give to Pachamama the heaviness that no longer serves you and trust she will give you back new life. That is the way it works. We don't have to understand or analyze it; only experience it. Each experience makes it easier to trust the next time.

It really can be easier than we imagine. Practice letting go and see how the universe conspires to assist you. One practice I find helpful is to imagine your current life exactly how you want it to be. What would it look like? How would it be? Every morning sit quietly in front of a lit candle and imagine your day going exactly how you would like it to go. Then release it to the universe (Divine Creator) and see what happens. If nothing else, it offers you the opportunity to recognize what really matters to you.

The more you connect with nature, the elements and your inner self, the more you will learn to trust that the divine is assisting you, offering you opportunities to choose life, simplicity, happiness and magic.

CHAPTER TEN

HARMONY

the third rite

In the Harmony Rite, seven different archetypes are transmitted into the chakras. This transmission helps the recipient to connect with the power of each archetype (the organizing principles of the universe) and their own energy centers. Starting with the first chakra, the archetypes are: the serpent, jaguar/puma, hummingbird, eagle/condor, Keeper of the Lower World (our subconscious), the Keeper of the Middle World (our waking world), and the Protector of the Upper World (our super conscious).

This Rite is given only to recipients who are willing to do the work to grow the seeds of these archetypes. These seeds germinate with fire, and the recipients are asked to perform a number of fire meditations to awaken them and help them grow. Afterward, each archetype helps combust the psychic sludge that has built up in the chakras, so the chakras can shine with their original light. This rite helps people to shed their past the way the serpent sheds her skin, all at once leaving the old behind.

After receiving this rite, the recipient needs to connect to each archetype individually for a period of at least two weeks, asking each archetype for guidance and the sharing of its wisdom and gifts. At the end of the two weeks, the initiate closes out that archetype and calls in the next one. The whole process takes a minimum of 14 weeks. If the recipients don't feel they connected to an archetype, they can call them in again.

The Harmony Rite is the only rite that requires homework. The 14 weeks working with the archetypes allows people to grow the seeds planted when they first receive the rite. In a sense, it helps grow the seeds of all the rites, by focusing one's attention on how the energy they received during the workshop continues to shift and change things inside them. This is how the magic of the Munay-Ki continues to operate.

There are many ways to work with the archetypes. The idea is to befriend each one so it can assist you in your life. As with any relationship, the more time and attention we give to it, the deeper it grows. Each morning you can light a candle and begin a meditation calling on the archetype you are working with that week. Focus on its energy and let it "speak" to you. During the day, open your consciousness to see how things going on in your life could be related to that archetype.

Alberto Villoldo wrote on the Munay-Ki website, "The great archetypes of our tradition are organizing principles of the universe. They are the forces that we call to create sacred space and they are the energy beings that have been planted as seeds in each of your chakras. It is important to remember that you have received them as seeds, they are pure potential – it is your own engagement with them and your relationship with them that will grow them into the powerful forces that inform your chakras in new ways. Instead of being exclusively informed by our histories and by our cultural prescriptions, these organizing principles of the Universe begin to organize our energy centers."[3]

---

[3]   For a detailed description of the archetypes see Appendix C

In February 2011, Christer and I taught three workshops in South Africa. Several participants had studied the Andean Tradition with Regis and Sergio in earlier years. Many commented on what a difference it made to them receiving the rites from both Christer and me, with such a beautiful harmony of the feminine and the masculine. Many of those people also commented to me how much softer my energy was in partnership with Christer than it had been when they knew me before.

When Christer and I do workshops together, both traveling and at Paz y Luz, I am the one who usually does most of the teaching. Christer, with his big strong presence holds the space without any ego-need to lead; quite the contrary, actually, because he prefers to assist. My style of teaching is inclusive and participatory so between the two of us there is a lovely balance of male and female in what some might call role reversals. The Harmony rite assists us with reaching this kind of balance, not only of the male/female but of all the dualities that sometimes prevent us from claiming our full power while retaining a gentle ease and stable presence.

Heather, who invited me to teach the Munay-Ki in South Africa, attended the first workshop I organized back in 1999 with Regis and Sergio. Because she knows so much about the Andean Spiritual Tradition, she was able to support the people who had done the Munay-Ki workshop in the Johannesburg/ Pretoria area where she lives. The other organizers, Linda in

Cape Town and Glenn and Cleone in Port Elizabeth, did the same with their communities.

People who had attended the workshops were then invited to come together every two weeks to share their experiences with one archetype and then do a fire ceremony to invite in the next archetype. In addition, people could share in between meetings with others in the community on a special Facebook page as well as by regular email.

From South Africa, I went to Mumbai, India, where I taught the Munay-Ki at a nearby hill station. Many from the India workshop joined Heather's Facebook group allowing them to share much useful information posted by the South Africans. This network also allowed people to share both similar and different experiences working with each archetype.

It was the first time I had taught four workshops on four consecutive weekends. Each group was unique in many ways but also shared a common experience of powerful magical changes within themselves. Feeling the energy of the rites passing from me to them week after week, in different settings, I was inspired to write this book. I realized, no matter what the culture or previous experience with Andean shamanism (or lack thereof), people have a profound connection with the energy of these rites. As of this writing, I have taught the Munay-Ki twenty four times in twelve countries on six continents. Soon I will teach it in Mexico, Hong Kong, Thailand and Kuala Lumpur as well as Peru. In my experience the "magic" is universal.

Carol, from San Antonio, Texas received the Munay-Ki at Paz y Luz in 2010. She shares some of her story here:

My friend told me about a book she was read-ing entitled Cusco: the Gateway to Inner Wisdom *by Diane Dunn. I looked Diane up online and found Paz y Luz, her healing place in Peru and the seminars offered there. I was particularly drawn to receiving the Munay-ki Rites. As soon as I read about them, without knowing the details, I knew that I had to go to Peru to receive the rites and meet Diane!*

During the past year after receiving the rites I have felt subtle changes in my day to day life and in my work as a massage therapist and Reiki practitioner. I do not adver-tise yet an increasing number of new clients are coming to me for healing work versus massage therapy. Additionally, I have been attracted to increase my own spiritual work which has resulted in regular meditation time and meet-ing more like minded people.

The one rite that I feel impacted me most is the Harmony Rite. After I left Paz y Luz I was charged with spending two weeks with each of the seven archetypes that had been transmitted into my chakras. What an awesome next 14 weeks I had spending intimate time with the ser-pent, jaguar/puma, hummingbird, eagle/condor, keeper of the Lower World (our unconscious), Keeper of the middle world (our waking world) and the Protector of the Upper World (our super conscious).

I spent many hours with each archetype and connect-ed with each of the energies. I began a new routine when going to work. When I go into my office for massage and Reiki, I now begin by lighting four candles for the four directions and call in the seven archetypes that then come and have a palpable presence in the room.

The archetype whose presence I feel the most is the

jaguar/puma. I can feel her walking the perimeter of the office while in session. Additionally during the sessions, the temperature in the room rises significantly and clients experience lasting healings on physical, spiritual and emotional levels.

The Harmony Rite and the work with the archetypes have helped many of my students connect in a deeper way to the power in all the Rites and to utilize that power in their everyday lives.

CHAPTER ELEVEN

AIR

The Air, a subtler element than Earth or Water, purifies and enlightens us. It is the element associated with knowledge, communication and connection. Air is the most basic and primary element of our existence. As we emerge from our mother's wombs we begin life with our first intake of air and we leave this earthly plane when we expel our last breath. And for every minute of every day of every year in between, we are sustained, nurtured, and purified by Air.

I was told that most human beings only use ten percent of the capacity of their lungs to breathe. Yet Air, through our breath, is one of the best healing regulators we have at our disposal. If we take three deep breaths in and out, we can relax away anger, tension, fear and other heavy, energy-sapping emotions. Intentional deep breathing can also relieve physical pain in the body.

Air is the primary conductor of communication. When we speak, it is air passing through us that allows our words to have sound. It is air that allows those words to be delivered and heard by those around us. Microphones, stereo speakers, radios, telephones, televisions all use the airwaves to deliver their sound and image. And in our generation, we have the most amazing technological use of the airwaves to date: the Internet and World Wide Web.

Imagine it – millions of messages and downloaded information flying through the airwaves in split seconds continuously throughout the day, every day, rarely missing their intended destination. There is something innate built into the system that moves messages in the quickest most direct route. If the most probable and direct route is blocked for some reason, the message is immediately transferred to the next most direct route and continues in this fashion until it reaches its desired destination. This happens without anyone working on a message-by-message basis to decide which is the most direct and open route and how it should be sent there. It just goes there in a split second.

The Internet is not only a wonderfully practical way of communication but an apt metaphor for our own ability to utilize Air and energy, not only for communication, but to discover ways of knowing we have only begun to tap. I imagine some internet-like network in the universe – the one that is always conspiring to assist us – that takes our clear intention, our stated desire, and shoots it out toward manifestation in the most direct route. If the intentions of others should block the most direct route then another is found and the desire continues on its path.

Air is energy and moves freely through time and space. When we know Air, travel with it, move on its wings, then we can also tap into its deep wisdom and knowledge of the ages. It broadens our perspective. The more we learn to know and work with this energy, the stronger power we will have to be instruments of transformation in our own lives and the world at large.

To learn from the Air, become more conscious of your breathing. Breathe more deeply and more slowly. Feel your breath filling all the areas of your body, not just your lungs. Imagine this energy entering your system, purifying all your organs and expanding your consciousness.

If you have a place you can go outside on a hilltop or a mountain, sit and meditate there. Feel the breeze on your face and your skin. Call the wind and see if it comes to you. Engage in conversation with the wind, with the Air. Give thanks for its life-giving breath, its refreshing breeze. Imagine you are part of this vast cosmic internet and ask for assistance with your ability to communicate with it and through it. Say to the wind, "Expand my consciousness. Amplify my awareness. Elevate my vibration so I may see and know as you see and know."

In June 2010, I taught a Munay-Ki workshop in northern Italy. After we finished I was flying high from the energy and magic experienced by our wonderful group. The Air was cool and crisp high in the western Alps, overlooking snowcapped mountains. Irene, who organized and translated the workshop, took me to a nearby town with an ancient site that had markings many believe were from extraterrestrials. We climbed up on the rocks and connected with the energy in this special place. As the wind blew strongly, I was called to lay belly-down on a specific rock to meditate. During my meditation I energetically connected with some beings who began to speak about the work I was doing with the Munay-Ki. They were so present I could almost see them floating above me. They told me my work was important preparation for what was coming. They would contact me when the time was right for me to work with them inter-dimensionally. Christer had always been much more interested than me in connecting with the cosmic beings, so I asked them if Christer could also be involved. They laughed at me as if I was missing the inside joke. "Christer is your bridge and your guide", they told me.

More and more of us are beginning to discover other ways of knowing and the vastness of our potential to know and communicate, to send and receive information, to send and receive love and light and healing. This potential is beyond our mind's capacity to hold because these other ways of knowing are not centered in our mind/brain, but rather in our heart/soul/spirit. The language is not verbal; it is image and energy. It's an understanding we have when we look at a painting or have a vision during a meditation. Perhaps we can describe it with words but we can't fully capture the experience or the knowledge we derive from the experience because the knowing is not something that happens solely with our mind or our emotions. It is an integrated experience we have with all levels of our being.

When I first learned to work with the four elements and nature, it seemed strange to me – lying on the ground, hugging a tree, or meditating with my feet in the water. I felt a bit self-conscious. However, the more I developed my relationship with the elements, the more I began to know and experience things on deeper levels. I began to know what the elements know, to learn from them.

Air is the element of expansion and acquiring a broader perspective. Imagine yourself in a closet or a small room of your house. Imagine if the world was only what you could see and touch. Now imagine you could lift the roof off your house and hover above it. Not only could you see all the rooms of your house but also the neighborhood and other people around it. As you move farther up you can see the whole city, the region. We can spend a lot of time rearranging the furniture in our house or we can expend the same effort shifting the energy in such a way we improve the condition of the whole region, which includes our house but is not limited to it.

For example, Nelson Mandela was a political prisoner in South Africa for 27 years, where he lived in a small dingy cell with few material objects. He could have narrowed his perspective to the confines of that cell and become an embittered man. But he made other choices. He expanded his perceptions to imagine the impossible. He refused to be bound by the limits his captors placed on him. Eventually, he was able to convince them that it was better for everyone to negotiate a form of power sharing that acknowledged the humanity of the oppressed majority.

Living in Johannesburg during that amazing transition period (1990–1999), I experienced the profound shift in people's feelings and beliefs that went beyond any logical rational explanation. That shift transformed not only the government and political system in South Africa, but also changed the way people felt about themselves and treated one another.

That kind of shift in collective consciousness is what is happening today around the world. The more we use the Air to expand our perception and awareness, the more able we will become to bring about the great transformation that the Inka prophecies tell us is just within our grasp. The codes within the Munay-Ki initiation Rites are assisting us to be instruments of that change. The element Air helps us utilize those codes to manifest this new reality.

CHAPTER TWELVE

SEER

the fourth rite

The Seer Rite installs filaments of light extending from your visual cortex in the back of your head to your third eye and heart chakras. This practice awakens your ability to perceive the invisible world. When receiving the Seer Rite, five extra cerebral pathways of light are installed that connect the visual cortex with the third eye in a "crown of light". Likewise, a "necklace of light" is activated from your heart chakra to the visual cortex. This awakens your "inner seer" and your ability to perceive the world of energy and Spirit. It helps you to see and know, not only from your analytical mind but more importantly from your heart and your intuitive perception.

There are shamans in the Andes, known as *q'awacs* who do coca leaf[4] readings to divine people's past/present/future lives. In Quechua q'awac means to see. The Seer Rite acts as bridge between western physiological science and this type of mysterious energetic knowing. It connects the visual cortex of the brain with the third eye and the heart center. By "turning on" these filaments of light, the recipient is able to perceive energy, to understand the world and oneself in a deeper and multidimensional way.

---

[4] Coca is a sacred plant in the Andes. The seeds and the leaves are used in ritual offerings. The leaves are chewed for energy, healing and inner vision;, brewed in a tea to help with high altitude symptoms; and also "read" by trained shamans who use them to give advice and even change the outcome of certain situations.

Even though the Seer Rite activates this ability in us, we need to practice using this alternative way of seeing and knowing. The ability to see in this new way is enhanced the more we utilize it.

Here at the Paz y Luz Healing Center, I offer Andean Energy Healing sessions. I put stones from the sacred river on the face and body of the patient. Then I work with the energy above and around the body. As I do this, I connect with that energy to see if there are blocks needing to be cleared. I sense certain issues about the person that could be causing them problems. We process together afterwards what they experienced and what I perceived.

Since first receiving this Rite in June 2007, my perception has increased. Sometimes I hear myself telling the patient things I was not even conscious I knew before the words came out of me.

I received the Rites for the first time only a few days before I met Christer. It is hard to say how much the rites had to do with our connection and the openness I felt with him, since there are many other factors which could have brought us together. But one vision I had four months after we met was particularly interesting.

Christer was still living in Sweden but was setting in motion his plans to move to Pisac to help me run Paz y Luz. We had agreed to a six-month trial period before he completely closed up his life in Stockholm. We spoke to each other almost every night sharing our hopes and visions. One morning during my meditation, I saw us getting married. Literally *saw* us. It was eight months in the future on June 26, 2008, my parents' 60th wedding anniversary. We were in the Hamptons (New York) standing barefoot on green grass in a circle with a small group of people. My friend Susanmerrie was officiating.

It is unusual for me to see the future but this was so clear and detailed I knew it hadn't come from my analytical mind. I was surprised because I didn't think I would ever get married again, having done it once (unsuccessfully) in my early 20s. I noted the vision but then let it go. That night when Christer and I were speaking with each other, he mentioned to me he had thought about us getting married and wondered how I felt about that! Christer was also married in his 20s and divorced ten years later. He had lived with the mother of his youngest daughter for many years without any interest in marrying again. So it was a bit odd for both of us to be discussing the subject at this early stage of our relationship. I shared with him my vision and he seemed delighted by it.

As I have said before, our six-month trial period was full of challenges so we both put that vision on the back burner. Christer decided he wanted to continue living with me in Peru but marriage seemed a long way off for both of us. We were planning to go to New York together in June for the weekend celebration of my parents' 60th anniversary. The 26th, their actual anniversary, was a Thursday so the family party wouldn't start until the 27th.

Christer had gone back to Sweden at the end of May to close up his apartment and his life there. I would travel to Stockholm in mid-June to meet the rest of his family I hadn't met on my first visit. In the meantime, I had arranged with my brother to stay at his house in the Hamptons a few days before the party for my parents.

I had let go of the wedding vision I had months before but found it interesting we would be in the Hamptons on that date. One night in early June Christer called me from Sweden and suggested we get married on June 26 in the Hamptons! After all the messages I received during our Gathering that April, that I needed to marry Christer, I happily said yes, let's do it.

Our actual wedding was exactly as I had seen it, barefoot on the lawn at my friend Leslie's house in Bridgehampton with Susanmerrie officiating and a small circle of friends and family surrounding us.

The ability to see the unseen world is a blessing but not necessarily always pleasant. I gave the rites to my dear friend Wendy in April 2008 just before the Gathering held at Paz y Luz to Envision, Experience and Manifest a new world. She writes:

> I was unaware at first of the power of the rites because I had not had any profound experiences during the transmissions. However, at the Gathering two events occurred that gave me a clue to the transformational energy of the rites, particularly the Seer Rite.
>
> During the Gathering, Jamee took each of us on a wonderful light body journey. This was accomplished with the rest of the group chanting and shaking rattles as well as six people lifting the light body out of the physical body to travel the globe. I knew I had past lives in Italy and the Middle East. I was determined to visit those places during

my journey. I did indeed get a glimpse of both areas as well as the American Southwest while I traveled. It was very enjoyable and I felt light (although a little spacey) when I came back to my body.

Later in the day, Diane did a lovely meditation with the group describing a bubble of light in which we would each travel to some beautiful location.

Only I didn't.

I found myself looking at tanks and barbed wire. Everything felt cold and bleak; there was an air of desperation surrounding everything. I was in a cave in this place, chilly and dank. I tried to leave the cave but kept being pulled back in. It was so horrible. I wanted to leave with every fiber of my being but seemingly could not escape.

I could hear Diane speaking gently and lovingly but I could not make it back and began to panic, thinking I had somehow gone over the edge and lost my mind. I had never had any experience like this before and didn't know what to do.

Luckily, a bug crawled onto my arm and some part of my brain responded, "I don't want that bug to bite me." I reached over to shoo the bug away and when my right hand touched my left arm I came back into my body and knew I would be fine.

I realized later I had stated an intention in the Light Body Journey to visit areas of my past life in Italy and although nothing special happened at the time, the Seer Rite perceived an opportunity to open my vision to a traumatic experience that needed to be healed. I had seen things with a frightening clarity and physicality.

I have worked with that vision in the ensuing years to understand the past life patterns that have held me captive in this lifetime. The Seer Rite facilitated that.

Brigitte from Belgium, received the Munay-Ki in Holland in April 2007. She was the first in Belgium to pass the Munay-Ki on to others. She writes:

> *Today I can see that my little snowball became a mountain. I have initiated over 300 people and still today I keep passing the Rites on to others in Belgium, Switzerland and Greece. I pass them on with my creativity and from my heart.*
>
> *When I give the Rites to others my whole body is warm, my eyes "see" and my heart is open. I am in this sacred space of peace, where no harm can be done. It fills me with light from all sides.*
>
> *I can see the many helpers around me as the hands that will touch every person. In the sacred space I see with different eyes, with different colors and I can see the connection with the people and with everything that is.*

Mary received the Rites from me in 2008 during our first Full Circle workshop. She teaches them in Ireland where she lives. She wrote:

> *The Seer Rite opens me up continually to a more grand way of "seeing". In the past years after receiving the rites, many many things in my life have been highlighted, changed, amplified. This Rite somehow has given me permission to be more awake to the seeing and knowing that has always been a part of me but which was disallowed by the conditions into which I was born – still disallowed in certain areas. I feel now there is a time and place for the communicating of "knowing" that is so clear at times.*

Seeing is a grand responsibility, a responsibility to self and to the earth and to other. But it also comes with a side note, a side note to be gentle and kind to those others who have not yet opened that perception. Kind but not hiding, gentle but strong with a sense of pride, a not being afraid to stand in the energy of this knowing and being acutely aware of the effect it has on the surrounding others. Sometimes a great emotional, energetic tornado follows. I do love the calm after the storms. I am a catalyst for growth and change, I know this. The rites and the experiences of Peru have allowed me to own more fully this knowing.

This rite opens you up to new ways of seeing and knowing. It also helps you understand yourself better. Like the exercises with the Air element, this rite expands your consciousness and teaches you to trust your intuition. There are many new frequencies broadcasting through the airwaves. The Seer Rite helps you tune into these new frequencies to amplify your inner wisdom. It opens you to possibilities previously inaccessible.

CHAPTER THIRTEEN

WISDOMKEEPER

the sixth rite

The Wisdomkeeper's Rite connects you to a lineage of luminous beings from the past and the future. This rite is associated with the snow-capped mountains, the place where humans meet God. In the Andean tradition, the mountains are referred to as *apus*, which really means the spirit of the mountain. Each apu has a name and a personality; the higher the mountain, the more powerful is the apu. The Wisdomkeepers call on the energy of the apus to assist them.

This rite helps you to step outside of time, to become steeped in the magic of the medicine teachings and taste infinity. The Wisdomkeeper Rite helps you heal your inner masculine, just as the Daykeeper Rite helps heal your inner feminine. It helps you connect to your inner wisdom and the mystery teachings of non-linear time and invisibility. It assists you to enter the world of energy, bringing wisdom and joy, eliminating suffering. It brings the secret into the light – the wisdom to know we are the Universe, we are Source.

In the Traditional form, the energy of this rite is called the *Altomisayoq*. It has been passed down from shamans to their apprentices in the high Andes for thousands of years. When you receive this rite and learn to give it to others, you are connecting with this lineage in a very powerful way.

When I invited Munay-Ki practitioners to share their experiences with me of how they found the Munay-Ki to be magical, I received many responses related to this rite.

Louisa, from California wrote:

The Munay-ki stirred something so deep inside of me... a knowing... a remembering so holy. This "knowing" I think is shared by many people across the planet earth at this time. It is a remembering of something we knew long ago but forgot.

I learned the Munay-Ki in Joshua Tree California where people came together from all over the world. It was in the conference room in Joshua Tree where I first felt all of the spirits that had ever lived on that particular desert site. Suddenly I could feel the presence of an ocean, a forest, of ancient bacteria and of large mammals that had gathered for the giving of the Wisdomkeeper Rite. This rite has the ability to connect people not based on religion, culture, profession or spoken language but to connect us at the level of the soul, to link us to that deep knowing that we are one with all that has been and all that will ever be. This Rite is the bridge to the divine inherent inside of each of us. Thank you to the ancients for knocking at our door and for helping us remember who we are.

Steen, from Denmark wrote:

After receiving the Wisdomkeeper Rite, I experienced a big leap in my own evolution. The development occurred in several areas around me and my life. In meetings with other people, I could sense a strong energy. I was able to express myself with a new sense of freedom, to be truly myself without worrying what others might say, even if my views might differ from that of the majority. I could dare to be me.

At the same time I experienced a very different and

*enhanced intuition, so that I immediately recognized
when someone was not speaking the truth or had a hidden
agenda. I also had glimpses of being able to see energies in
nature. One day I stood and looked out over some wooded
hills. The area is esoteric, known as Denmark's throat
chakra, so therefore has a strong energy. While I stood and
enjoyed the view over the hills in the distance, and the
blue sky, I suddenly saw a silver edge between the horizon
line and sky, and just at this location. I understood immediately that I was seeing the Earth's energy.*

In September 2010, I went to the Lofoten Islands in north-ern Norway to teach the Munay-Ki. These islands are north of the Arctic Circle with some of the most stunningly beautiful landscape I have ever seen. How I ended up there was magical in itself. Some months before, I received an email from Lilian who wrote after reading my first book. She is a Dutch woman of many talents who moved to Lofoten ten years ago, mainly as a music teacher. She enjoyed the midnight sun, she told me, but wanted to live in Lofoten all year especially to experience the winter darkness as well as the summer sun. She commented in her email she had always wanted to come to Peru.

I wondered at the time how she came to have my book since almost all the people who wrote me bought the book while they were visiting Peru. When I wrote her back I said I had been to Oslo but not northern Norway and would love to come if she wanted to organize for me to teach the Munay-Ki there. "And by the way, how did you get my book?" She wrote back she'd be honored to organize the workshop and told me she found my book in a second hand book store in Lofoten! How my book made it to the Arctic Circle and into the hands of Lilian I didn't know, but I was sure it was a sign we should meet.

Teaching the Munay-Ki in Lofoten was indeed a very special experience for me. Working with the elements in that stark, primal and powerful place was truly awe inspiring. The temperatures were chilly with every kind of weather you could imagine – rain, clouds, sunshine and mist, but it all added to the experience of being profoundly connected with nature and creation.

This is what Lilian wrote of her experience:

> *On the whole, I feel that there has been a kind of opening in me, I am much more grounded in my spiritual being. Much more convinced about who I am, which is wonderful. "Something" has opened up and made me feel more integrated with myself.*
>
> *When I received the Wisdomkeeper Rite, I saw this group of lightworkers standing around me, waiting for me to take my place among them. And there was a place for me! I knew most of these people already: some being deceased family members and some I don't know where I knew them from, but they were familiar all the same. It was very moving and beautiful, but most of all empowering, because I felt too that I was one of them.*
>
> *Then, a couple of days after receiving the rites, I gave a client of mine a shiatsu-treatment (Japanese energy-body-work). This person literally asked me: "Wow, what have you been doing?" as he felt a great difference in my approach. I too, felt the energy flowing very, very easily and it has been like this ever since.*

When Christer and I went to South Africa in February 2011 to teach the Munay-Ki, he commented how strongly he resonated with this rite. Calling on the Wisdomkeepers before giving the rite he would feel a powerful connection with them as if they were physically present.

The Wisdomkeeper Rite is the sixth rite given in the Munay-Ki. After receiving the other five Rites, usually people are ready to step into this new realm where the boundaries between the seen and the unseen are very thin. This rite assists us to step beyond time and space where alternative ways of seeing and knowing are active and accessible. As Judi points out below, this way of knowing can't be held in the thinking logical mind. It requires us to step into another dimension all the while keeping our feet on the ground and our hearts wide open.

Judi took the course taught by Christer and me in Port Elizabeth, South Africa in February 2011. She wrote:

> *The person I am today, eight weeks after receiving the Rites, is a completely different being to who I was before the workshop. Diane explained to us that the Rites are energetic transfers of wisdom. Intellectually in the moment I thought that made sense. It soon became apparent that there was no way that my mind could comprehend this energetic transfer of knowledge, because energetically, this knowledge expands over time through all four bodies, physically, mentally, emotionally and ethereally at the soul level.*
>
> *It sounds very romantic and wonderful, but the process itself can be difficult if blockages need to be removed or if one is energetically not in alignment. Although it was a bumpy ride for me at first, I now feel more aligned*

with my true nature. With it have come wisdom, love, compassion and insight. Receiving the Rites was a profoundly deep, powerful and moving experience in itself. The Presence of and connection to Spirit and the Earth has been tangible for me, and growing through my personal practice.

Receiving the Munay Ki Rites has given me a new sense of purpose on the planet. I feel more grounded, energetically aligned and charged. The future looks clear, the past released and the NOW a dynamic point of creation. I feel a sense of belonging and connection that I have never felt before. Thanks to that, I am able to give more fully, energetically contribute more valuably, while feeling a deep sense of peace.

The Munay Ki Rites have awakened my psychic ability to interact with nature. They have opened my heart to the Universal flow of Love. I feel safe, protected, I trust now. Earth and all her elements have become alive for me as has the interplay and inter-connectedness between the many dimensions and us as the family of humanity. I see the world through awakened senses and understand how important our contribution is individually as guardians and stewards on the planet.

Practicing the Munay Ki is empowering at many levels and a blessing to awaken the luminous one inside all of us. The greatest and most delightful benefit has been without a doubt the powerful connection I feel with Spirit and the Earth. The love and joy in my heart is over-flowing from this experience. This is a sacred gift of love and wisdom to all of humanity.

I agree with Judi that these rites are a gift to us at this very special time in our history. The Wisdomkeepers help us to connect to the energy of the apus who act like a bridge for us to enter into other dimensions, to see the world as the magical place it is, to tune in to the cosmic internet so we can begin to grasp the vastness of our reality. When we move beyond the material into the energetic we become so much more capable of co-creating our new world into being.

CHAPTER FOURTEEN

FIRE

Fire is the most powerful of all the elements, connected with love and passion and compassion. Fire sanctifies and transmutes. Fire changes coal into diamonds. Fire changes iron ore into gold. The power of Fire is alchemy. Transmutation. It has the power to change hate into love, darkness into light, ice into water, water into vapor. Working with Fire, we can learn how to transmute our anger and rage into peace and compassion.

The source of Fire on this planet is the Sun. For this reason, the sun was revered by the Inkas and many other indigenous traditions. The movement of the sun and the stars was followed closely by the ancient wise ones who knew our lives depended on this Fire-ball in the sky. That same spark of Fire, which exists inside us, is what gives us life and sustains us every day.

The Fire element is what enables us to dare, to move beyond our comfort zone in order to expand our horizons, our awareness, our consciousness. It is Fire that inspires us to be more than we think we are, to discover the wonders of being alive.

Fire burns away our fear, our rage, our shame and transmutes it into love and confidence. One of the best ways to connect with Fire is to catch the first ray of the sun as it rises each day. When the sun is low on the horizon, we can look directly into it without injuring our retinas. The power of the sun as it breaks the horizon goes straight into our hearts, energizing our whole being, sanctifying any dark corners, releasing any fear residing in us.

With great anticipation, I love sitting in dawn's gray light, waiting for the sun to come up. This open eye meditation is enhanced as I watch the sky changing colors, from gray to pink and orange and purple. The wonder of where and when the sun will pop up brings me back to the simple joy I knew in my childhood when so much of nature was a source of delight for me. The actual moment when the sun breaks the horizon is breathtaking and awesome. The birds join the celebration with their chirps and songs. And it happens every day! Try it.

Another powerful practice is to make a fire outside as the sun is setting. Stare into the flames and let the Fire within you connect with the flames. Listen to the sounds the Fire is making. Let the Fire converse with you. Take a small stick and with your intention, put into the stick all that you want to transmute, as well as what you want to manifest. When it feels right to you, put the stick in the fire, trusting your intentions will be made manifest. Let the Fire inspire you.

By working with the Fire, and all the elements of nature, we increase the awareness of our senses – our five physical senses (sight, touch, taste, smell and hearing), as well as our sixth sense (perception). These practices will open our awareness in the routine of our everyday lives. We will learn to see beyond the familiar. This knowledge is held in the heart and the soul and the cosmos, beyond time and space, not only in the mind.

Fire is the element of the Heart. Living from the heart is becoming more and more crucial during this time of great transition. Like the element itself, our ability to keep our hearts open is subtle. There is a very fine line sometimes between love and fear, passion and rage.

On a trip to South Africa with Christer in 2010, a year before teaching the Munay-Ki in Port Elizabeth, I had another opportunity to experience how trapped, frustrated and angry we both can feel when our hearts are closed, and how everything lightens when we can open them up again.

It was a beautiful January summer and I was really looking forward to sharing with Christer two of my favorite places when I lived in South Africa in the 90s: the romantic Quiet Mountain Lodge and the Pilanesberg Game Reserve. However, the morning we set out for the game reserve, I received an upsetting email from Paz Y Luz, plus I was getting a cold.

When I asked Christer how to handle the situation at our center in Peru, he said, "Just forget about it." His response felt harsh and dismissive so I decided to turn inward with my eyes closed. Ten minutes into our 90-minute drive, I was jolted awake when Christer hit a pothole, which bent the tire rim on our rather small rental car. Christer was irritated with himself but I felt he was irritated with me. He was driving because I wasn't feeling well and he wasn't used to driving on the left side of the road.

We drove the rest of the way in silence. After arriving, I'd hoped Christer's mood would improve. This time it seemed like he was the one trapped inside of his own closed heart. I tried to get in but encountered only the steel gate. Instead of pausing to enjoy the animals when we spotted them, he kept driving as if he were on his way somewhere. When I lived in South Africa, this was my favorite game park and I was really looking forward to sharing the experience with him but the mood in the car was far from pleasant. The weather was getting hotter and our air conditioning was not functioning very well.

We stopped at a picnic site to have lunch. I was trying to lighten things up but to no avail. I felt stuck, finding him unavailable and difficult to be near. I kept asking myself for the lesson and searched for a way to take care of myself given the circumstances. I chose non-engagement (which in this case was a kissing cousin to closed-heartedness). The shade of the picnic site was so pleasant compared to the heat in the car (physical and emotional), I was stunned that Christer wanted to leave even before I was finished eating. He said he wanted to go back to our guest house.

Part of me was happy at the thought of being back at Quiet Mountain, our beautiful retreat. I longed to jump in the pool to cool off in more ways than one. But I was also deeply disappointed that the "highlight of our trip" was such a disaster. Little did I know what still awaited us!

Christer drove through the park faster than the 20 km speed limit allowed, a man on a mission. I said a little prayer to God, asking for a sign: "If we see a giraffe, I'll take it as a sign that everything will be OK." I had to smile, just as we were exiting the park, there was one lone giraffe on Christer's side of the car.

Things got much worse however, before they got better. Once we were back on the main road home, we got a flat tire, the one with the bent rim. It was about 100 degrees in the sun as we tried to figure out how to change the tire. I was reading out of the manual trying to cheer him up – a hopeless endeavor.

Just as we got the spare on the car, a nice man named Marius stopped to see if we were OK. The spare was barely bigger than a bicycle tire. Marius confirmed there was no town nearby to fix the tire so we decided to keep going. Christer was driving painfully slow, mostly on the shoulder of the highway.

Within 15 minutes he hit a small pot-hole exactly on that little spare and it popped like a balloon. Unbelievable. We had a cell phone with us so I called the rental car company. It was about 4 p.m. by then. We had been on hold for so long, when the agent came back on the line with a solution, our phone disconnected because we ran out of minutes. We waited in the blazing sun for them to call back.

In the meantime, Marius drove past again. He offered to take the first tire to a place he knew about 40 minutes away, to repair it. Finally the agent in Pretoria called to say he would send a new car but it would take two hours to reach us. I asked him to call John at Quiet Mountain to say we would be late for dinner.

Christer angrily declared, "There is no God." And he really meant it. I'd never seen him so down hearted. I tried to keep my sense of humor and cheer him up. No luck. At 7:45, now completely dark, Marius arrived and our Good Samaritan had the original tire back on the car in short order. The new car arrived shortly after that.

I didn't really know the way back to Quiet Mountain and for some reason John, who had called us several times earlier, hadn't called for 40 minutes. Every decision to turn or not was sheer torture, Christer treating me as if I were his worst enemy.

At 8:30 John finally called. We had made a wrong turn and had to go back. We were now on small country roads with no street lights. John called us every 5-10 minutes until we found a landmark we both knew.

We got home at 9:30 p.m. both ready to strangle the other. At dinner I jokingly said, "Tomorrow we can talk about all the things we learned from this experience." Christer responded dryly, "I learned two things: 1. there are lovely people out there that help you; 2. You and I can't play on the same team."

That was the final straw for me. A façade of pleasantry and understanding fell away and the anger and steely heart I'd been protecting behind closed doors since the morning, came out with vengeance. I gave him all the examples how I had supported him, where as he hadn't supported me at all in my illness or my desire to show him one of my favorite places. I stormed out of the dining room and I locked the bedroom door behind me hoping he would ask John for another room. So much for our romantic retreat.

I took a bath in the deep antique footed tub, lit a candle and played Roy Hargrove on my iPod. I tried to relax but didn't succeed very well. I knew my heart was closed but I couldn't get it to re-open. While I was in the bath, Christer used a spare key to get in the room. He was "sleeping" on the far side of our king size bed. With my heart now locked in a prison of my own making, I couldn't bear the idea of reaching out to him and didn't think there was much chance he would apologize to me. I lay with my back to him on the other side of the bed.

Knowing I could spend the next day poolside at Quiet Mountain or using the internet in the main lounge got me through the night – that and seriously considering a divorce. The Munay-Ki magic must have been working on me as I slept because sometime in the early morning, I woke up with the odd idea I could reach over and touch my husband's bare back which wasn't so far away. An inner dialogue began between my higher self and my wounded inner child. "Go ahead. Touch him." "No, I can't." "Yes, you can. Just reach out and touch him." "I can't." "Oh come on – if he pushes you away, you'll be no worse off than you are now."

With all the Fire-power daring I could muster, I reached out and lightly touched his back. He moved a little closer, still with his back to me. I also moved closer, my chest to his back. We embraced that way for a few minutes. I could feel both our hearts opening. Remarkable. Soon he turned around, as if he knew it was safe again. "I'm sorry", he said in such a sweet genuine way. "Me too." We smiled, hugged and kissed. Hearts once more open and connected. All the heaviness of the day before resolved once again in a magical flash. Passing through hurt and vulnerability, we could once again return to love. That's the magic of an open heart and the transmutative power of the Fire.

CHAPTER FIFTEEN

EARTHKEEPER

the seventh rite

The Earthkeeper Rite connects you to a lineage of archangels that are guardians of our galaxy. They're reputed to have human form and be as tall as trees. The Earthkeepers, who are stewards of all life on the Earth, come under the direct protection of these archangels and can summon their power when they need to in order to bring healing and balance to any situation.

This Rite corresponds in the tradition with the *Kuraq Akulleq* initiation. In Quechua, kuraq akulleq means the elder who chews coca, or the wise master who knows many things. They are the ones who have the wisdom of experience and have mastered the art of working with energy. When they summon the wind or call on the rain, the elements of nature respond. The communities turned to these wise ones for advice and counsel. They are the bridge between heaven and earth, the mediators between divine and human.

When I first received this rite in 2007, I felt the energy shiver through my body, akin to an electric shock. It was a sweet sensation. It was as if this lineage of wise ones were knocking at my door, letting me know they were there to assist me. That energy, the connection I felt with the lineage, was what guided me to teach the Andean Tradition in my own way, ultimately using the Munay-Ki Rites so others could feel their support as well.

Historically, this rite was given after many years of experience practicing the tradition. But we are living in a very special moment of history where everything is speeding up. Our ability to receive and share this energy has increased dramatically since 2007. Our consciousness is vibrating at a higher frequency. So when we receive these energy transmissions, we are much better able to integrate the energy and utilize it to bring healing and balance into our lives.

When Christer first moved to Paz y Luz late in 2007, we began to push each other's buttons quite regularly. The issues seemed somewhat territorial as I tried to create space in my house for him. Sometimes I became obsessed with the proper location of things in the kitchen, for example. I'm sure it was much more about creating space in my life, than it was about the order of things in my house. For Christer it was about finding comfort in a place that was new, that wasn't yet his.

Our love continued to bloom and grow, even as we triggered things in the other, helping us to heal. From our first car rental fiasco in St. Lucia to the flat tire trauma in South Africa, as well as here at home, whenever situations are the most challenging, I can feel the Earthkeepers watching over us, as our doubts and fears ebb and flow, and old wounds are given a chance to mend.

In January 2010, the sacred river outside our door flooded, bringing two feet of water and mud into our house and half that into our hotel rooms. Christer and I were on holiday in South Africa when it happened. The volunteer looking after the hotel, evacuated the premises and left the area. Our new manager who was supposed to start the following month decided not to come. Two women who had committed to run our new restaurant changed their minds.

When I got the news on the other side of the hemisphere, my immediate emotional response was one of betrayal and abandonment, not only by our potential colleagues but also by Pachamama and the Earthkeepers. Christer received the news with a calm steady strength that provided a container which allowed me to process my feelings without fuelling them. Twenty-four hours after hearing about the flood, our neighbors informed us that the water had receded and our house was still standing.

Tears poured out of me releasing the tension as Christer stood over me like a guardian. It was then my emotions shifted from anger at the ones who left to gratitude for our local staff who stayed and had already begun cleaning things up. I remembered that the element Earth cleanses and the Water washes. The Earthkeepers in fact were doing their job cleansing and transforming on all levels – physical, emotional and spiritual. Christer's steady countenance and gentle loving strength was such a comfort to me.

We celebrated Thanksgiving that year at Paz y Luz, inviting all our friends, neighbors and guests for a big meal with turkey and all the trimmings. There were 28 people from 19 countries including my parents, my brother Dennis and his wife Sharon. We sat in a circle each one sharing what we were thankful for that year. Surrounded by so many people who had helped us during the flood and as we made repairs, Christer so beautifully expressed our gratitude for all the care and support we received. I felt gratitude to Pachamama and the Earthkeepers as well.

The Earthkeepers help us shift our consciousness to see life from a broader perspective, which opens us up to so many new possibilities. Sylvia, who invited Christer and me to teach the rites in Bariloche, Argentina, came to Peru for the "Deepening the Munay-Ki" retreat I offer every year. During the five days of this retreat, we share our experiences with Munay-Ki. We also go to four sacred initiation sites in Cusco and the Sacred Valley, where mountain shamans received the rites for many generations. These sites are unknown to most tourists. I work with Don Francisco and his wife Dona Juanita who give us the lineage rites in the traditional way with their *mesas,* sacred stones wrapped in a traditional woven cloth.

On the fourth day of the retreat, we go to an old temple with a carved chakana altar. There Francisco and Juanita give us the Kuraq Akulleq initiation with their mesas.

Sylvia's husband Jimmy had been very sick for more than a year. She shared this story with the group when we returned from receiving this rite.

> *We got there, and I sat down on a rock and found myself meditating. So I went with it and there was Jimmy, his back against the rock with a kind of tunic on, hands outstretched, with a ceremonial dagger in his chest. He wasn't a bit put out; in fact he had a smile on his face. So I went up to him, took him by the hand, and walked him to the tunnel. We parted; he waved, smiled, and turned and walked away. As did I. And connecting us was this tube of energy of light which stretched as we walked in opposite directions. Powerful to say the least. I had been trying to talk to Jimmy energetically for some time, to let*

him know it was OK not to hang on to life endlessly if he really wants to go. This time I managed, quite beautifully.

The course to learn the Munay-Ki Rites doesn't teach you shamanic techniques or train you to perform other rituals and practices of the tradition. There is other training available for that. What Munay-Ki does is open us up to the vast potential within us and to the many possibilities that exist beyond our material practical reality of linear time and space. The rites tune us in to alternative frequencies.

This rite in particular, and how it has been given in the last 15 years or so, has caused some controversy among students and teachers of the Andean tradition. Until 2007 and the birth of the Rites to Come, the Kuraq Akulleq initiation was the ultimate rite. Like its name explains, traditionally it was given after many years of practice and experience. When Peruvian professionals and foreigners began learning the tradition from indigenous shamans, they eventually received this rite themselves. When they began teaching foreigners the tradition, this was the prize, you might say, for learning well and completing the full course of study.

Teachers each have their own style and form for teaching the tradition and their own organization, their own fees and their own length of study. My teachers for example, taught us using four levels of the Andean priesthood and within those four levels, there were six initiations in total, the last being the Kuraq Akulleq.

With each level some people would fall away, as more new initiates would start at level one. I received five of the six initiations over the nine years I worked with Regis and Sergio. Regis finally offered the Kuraq Akulleq initiation as part of a 18-day trip around Peru and Bolivia, eleven years after the first workshop I organized for him in 1999 in South Africa. Ten people from South Africa received it out of hundreds who had done the other levels over the years.

Alberto Villoldo has a school called Healing the Light Body. Through this school, he has been training people in shamanic healing practices for more than 20 years. One model he uses for some of his training is a medicine wheel and the four cardinal directions. At the end of the 4th direction (the East), students receive the Kuraq Akulleq rite.

In the mid-90s, Juan Nunez Del Prado, working with Elizabeth Jenkins, began leading groups of foreigners for a ten-day initiation journey to sacred sites in and around Cusco. All the lineage rites were given to the participants as part of that journey, culminating with the Kuraq Akulleq rite. Regis and Juan had both studied with a master shaman from Huasao named Don Benito years before so they knew each other and shared many teachings they had learned together. Regis had also studied with other masters so he drew his knowledge from several sources. They had much in common but chose to share the rites in different ways.

By 2000, when I moved to Cusco, there were many people who were leading groups, teaching the tradition and sharing the rites, often given to the foreigners by indigenous shamans who worked alongside the teachers and group leaders. Among different teachers and students there have been debates about whose way is more authentic, more appropriate, more valid. These debates continue and the Munay-Ki is often part of those discussions.

In 2009, Peggy from my Full Circle group and I had an interesting discussion about the use of mesas. The Full Circle included a Munay-Ki training to receive and give the rites using a Pi stone. It also included visiting four sacred initiation sites and receiving the lineage rites from Francisco and Juanita in the traditional way with their mesas. As part of the tradition, Francisco was giving each person a stone from the site to put in their mesa. Some of the people participating in the Full Circle were mesa carriers, having learned about the mesa from other training they had taken (like Peggy and me) but others were new to the tradition and didn't have a mesa. For these people, Francisco offered to help them start a mesa with special stones and a hand-woven manta cloth that they could buy from him.

Peggy was very distressed these people were getting a mesa without *earning* it. She said she had to work so hard and went through so much training. She felt Francisco just giving these other participants a mesa was somehow diminishing *her* mesa. I told her that her mesa represented her own journey and that it was valuable and powerful to her for that reason and didn't need to be compared to someone else's.

I feel the same way about receiving the Munay- Ki rites. Each way of teaching the tradition has its merits. Students have their own experiences during their training. Most often they learn what is important for them to learn. Juan Nunez, Albert Villoldo and others felt the time was right to share the initiation rites, including the Kuraq Akulleq, with as many people as possible to assist the coming of a new age. So they created ways for that to happen.

As I was thinking about this topic, I was reminded of a parable told by Jesus (recorded in Matt. 20:1-16) about laborers in the vineyard. Some workers were hired first thing in the morning and agreed to work all day for a silver coin. The owner then went out during subsequent hours collecting more workers. At the end of the day, some had worked many hours, others only a few but they were each paid the same silver coin. The ones who worked the longest were upset because they thought they deserved more than the ones who hadn't. The owner asked why they were upset because they had been given exactly what they had been promised.

Most biblical scholars interpret this story to mean that God's grace is unmerited rather than earned. Some people may say a certain teacher's training is worth more than another's, which of course may be true. But in the end, the initiation rites of the Andean tradition (including the Munay-Ki) are an energetic connection with higher consciousness and the Divine. There are techniques that can be taught to utilize that energy but the rites themselves are like God's grace which isn't earned by our worthiness, but given freely to assist humanity.

I didn't like that parable when I was young. I thought it was unfair, unjust. One should be paid what one earned, what one deserves. But now, after many years practicing Andean spirituality, I conclude we'd all be in big trouble if we got only what we earned or deserved. Then we would miss the magic, we'd miss the unconditional love of Divine Creator who gives sunshine and air to the good and bad alike. Fair or not, the rites are given to expand our consciousness – both personal and collective – so we can let go of what is fair and right to embrace love and beauty and acceptance instead.

We may not all be equal but we are all acceptable. Those who train people in the Andean Spiritual tradition do it differently. Their students have free will to choose where, when, how and with whom they wish to study and what they are willing to pay for that training. The choices made are not validated by negating the other options. The value is determined by how the teachings enable the students to improve their lives, and each life that their lives touch.

My life was greatly improved by what I learned from Regis and Sergio, and I am grateful to them for what they taught me. That grace continues with learning and teaching the Munay-Ki and working with Francisco and Juanita. It is the energy of the rites that opens us up – I can see that when I teach the Munay-Ki to others.

The Earthkeeper Rite especially guides me when I share the Andean tradition with others. The Earthkeepers are the ones who remind me how important it is we learn how to trust we are being guided and assisted during this time of great turmoil and change. They are the ones that keep us reaching for the sky with our feet firmly planted on the earth. They help us navigate when our usual compasses are spinning in all directions. We are indeed being looked after from a higher source. When we feel that energy inside us, we can trust it is at work in the world around us as well, no matter how chaotic things seem from our material practical vantage point. That's grace. That's the magic.

CHAPTER SIXTEEN

STARKEEPER

the eighth rite

The Starkeeper Rite is the first of the two "Rites to Come". It anchors you safely to the time after the great change that is said will occur on or around the year 2012. According to lore, when you receive this Rite, your physical body begins to evolve into that of *homo luminous.* The aging process is slowed down, your DNA is re-informed, and you become resistant to diseases to which you were once vulnerable.

After receiving this Rite, you may notice you no longer process events occurring in your life primarily at the physical level but rather, at the Spirit level. When you receive this rite, you acquire stewardship of the time to come and all future generations. It downloads the final codes for the new human into the luminous energy field and anchors you in the future NOW. It opens and connects you to all the future possibilities.

In the Starkeeper Rite, the energy is pulled in from the Star Beings and transmitted into each of the seven chakras, while recipients are lying down on their backs.

The energy of this rite corresponds to the *Mosaq Karpay* which in Quechua means new rite. Andean shamans began giving this rite to one another in 1992 as a way to recharge their shamanic abilities by connecting with the Star Beings from the constellation of the Pleiades during the annual Qoyllur Rit'i festival where traditionally they climb a high glacier mountain to bring down a chunk of holy ice.

For the last several years, they stopped taking ice because of the significant melting of the glacier, thought to be one of the signs indicating the imminent arrival of the taripaypacha.[5] This connection with the Star Beings was a way in the here-and-now to anchor themselves in the time-to-come.

I have been giving and receiving the Starkeeper Rite for several years and when giving it, I feel such a strong connection with the Star Beings who gifted us this special energy. They know who we really are, where and what we are evolving into, and call us into our higher selves at this very important time in our collective history. I can feel their energy entering my hand as I reach up to receive it and bring it down into each chakra of the person to whom I am giving the rite.

Many people feel this energy strongly. Here are a few descriptions of people's experiences with the Starkeeper.

Daz, from England now living in Peru, received this rite from Dani who learned the rites from me in 2009.

> *Lying down for the Starkeeper, Dani called in the energies from the heavens and Stars and she felt the energies of the serpent in the root, the planet Mars in the Sacral, the hummingbird in the Solar, the Eagle/Condor in the Heart, Archangel Gabriel in the Throat, Quetzacoatl in the third eye, and Archangel Michael in the Crown. Some of the big guns had come in and I felt so blessed. I certainly felt the energy of the third eye.*
>
> *But it wasn't until that night when I was about to fall asleep when somebody turned up the electricity in my body. I was just lying there, when this amazingly intense energy rose up inside and expanded out beyond my body. I felt like my light body at one stage was about to jump out*

---

5 The mythical new golden age spoken of in the Inka prophecies, preceded by upheaval on the planet

and leave the body. It was surreal. It lasted for about 10 minutes and then the energy started to retract and return to normal. I never fight these things. I really love to go with them. Something had changed in me that night for sure and I feel things have grown so much within me. I feel very different to the time before I received the Munay-Ki. The physical 'upgrades' can be quite intense at times, but so well worth it.

Jonna-Maria, who hosted me for a workshop in Copenhagen, Denmark in 2008, wrote:

For me the Munay-Ki was "coming home". These rites helped me get closer in touch with my own kernel. I can clearly feel the Healer in me, and from Harmony Rite I always use Huascar Inka when I work with clients or give talks. I love all the rites but my favorite is Starkeeper. It has more than anything, taught me that I am master of my own life.

Although I still enjoy having my angels and guides around me, I can even manifest things without calling on them now. Before, my grandchildren called the "parking angel" when we needed a parking space. Now they laugh when I say that they don't need to bother her because I can do it myself. When we need help with something, it has become a game where they ask, "Should we call an angel or can you do it, Grandma?" And I can do it myself much more frequently than before. I am so grateful to the Munay-Ki; the energy is now an important and integral part of me and my life.

Silvia is a Peruvian who has lived in South Africa since her twenties. She married a South African and raised her children there. She is a professional interpreter/translator of Spanish-English. She learned about the Andean tradition from my teachers Regis and Sergio, when she was asked to translate for a workshop they were teaching. She resonated deeply with the tradition of her ancestors. She learned the Munay-Ki in February, 2011 when Christer and I taught the workshop near Johannesburg. She writes:

During the Starkeeper Rite, I was the recipient of a powerful cosmic download; I was told to trust that the Andean lineage was present pouring ancient knowledge and energies in a column of light through my open crown chakra as well as a loving light directly into my sonko (heart), I do not have images or words in 3D attached to it, I felt as if I was flying in total freedom, I perceived Regis' smile, I perceived Regis' teachers' smiles and also Manco Capac's (Inka) smile, I felt the apus. I felt the stars. Was told that I was going to be guided to bring out and apply the appropriate knowledge and energies as necessary and to trust my intuition because Spirit was holding all that is.

I know the Munay-ki is working in me, reconnecting and enabling my DNA as part of the process into the time to come. Now I know it is the apus that will make the energies come together. I know the Starkeeper is a cosmic alignment of divine energy that will embrace my energy self if I have an open heart, a humble mind and a loving attitude of service.

Kathleen from New York, whom I met while she was staying with us at Paz y Luz, shared with me this beautiful story of her experience with the Starkeeper Rite:

"Starkeeper, Starkeeper". The words, and the soft sound of the voice delivering the words, whirled in the air and I had the feeling I would have a special relationship with this particular rite. I had received the previous seven rites over a period of two years and, although not fully understanding their meanings at the time of transmission, I slowly came to understand them as I came to experience them in my being and life. But this was not unusual for me. Like many, experience is the way I learn most completely and best.

I love all of the Munay-Ki rites but must admit that I have a certain affinity for the Starkeeper Rite. This rite, one of the 'rites to come', offers me energetic support so I may access information needed to help shift myself and others into new ways of thinking and being. These new ways of thinking and being are more in sync with the time of Pachakuti, or the great turning over of the earth, and beyond. I think of the Starkeeper as a sort of visionary in that she may appear to be a bit ahead of her time. She can travel to the stars and receive messages and information needed for the future. She can then work with that information in ways that are most suited to her, and share it so others may learn what they need to learn to transition and evolve during this exciting time on our planet.

As an artist, I tend to spend a lot of time in creative states. Some of these creative states can be similar to altered states, which are commonly engaged in for journeying and traveling outside of the body. The Starkeeper Rite enables one to journey to the stars for knowledge and wisdom. Perhaps she does this with intention from the outset, but perhaps it occurs effortlessly and spontaneously as in a dream simply by holding space for it in her awareness. As the

151

seed of this rite grew and developed in my system, I found myself having more non-ordinary experiences. Oftentimes, I sought to integrate these experiences by creating artistically. For me, it is easier to translate an experience of this nature in a way that is not confined to verbal language. I like to use color, shape, pattern and form to express what I need to express.

The Munay-Ki rites are beautiful and life-changing. They grow as we cultivate and nourish them; I imagine it similar to growing a plant. When I feed my plant, water her, give her sun, talk to her, and engage with her, she usually responds and grows. Active participation with the rite is essential for blossoming to occur. As blossoming occurs, the full potential of the rite can become manifest. When manifest, we begin to more fully understand the prophecy of that new kind of human being emerging who moves forward in peace and harmony with all of Life.

The true test of the power of these rites, along with my own Andean spiritual practice, came in a shocking way for me in June, 2011. Most of this book was written by then when Christer and I went to Florida to celebrate my Mom's 90th birthday with my family. Only these few chapters remained. I said to Christer before we left, "I have a feeling there is something else that hasn't happened yet that needs to go in the book." I thought it would be something to do with the workshops we were doing in Europe in August or maybe some planetary shift.

Little did I know what new insights were about to present themselves and what the cost would be. We flew up to Miami together on June 17th for the celebration of my mother's 90th birthday, and then drove 90 minutes north to Jupiter where my brother Dennis and his wife Sharon live. That night Christer and I went on a sunset cruise with the family, eating, drinking and catching up with everyone. My mom's siblings were there whom I hadn't seen in many years and who hadn't yet met Christer. It was a lovely evening which continued back at Dennis and Sharon's house.

The next morning when Christer and I were getting ready to leave our hotel, Christer had trouble breathing; when he passed out I called an ambulance. Christer went in and out of consciousness while the paramedics worked on him. We didn't know what was wrong. I called Dennis who lived only minutes away and he came to be with me. I felt so helpless.

On the way to the hospital, Christer's heart stopped. They inserted a breathing tube and pumped his chest to revive the heart. In the Emergency Room, this happened five more times over a 40 minute period. They determined he had a massive blood clot over both lungs which stopped the blood flow to his heart and brain.

After a few hours the doctors were able to dissolve the clot but there was major trauma to the brain and other organs. He was still alive but they were very concerned with his condition. The doctors decided to do a treatment that assists the brain by dropping the body temperature. During this procedure they paralyze the body so there is no movement. I was not allowed to be with him during this 36 hour process. He was moved to the ICU and I left the Emergency Room with my three brothers who had all been keeping vigil with me.

I had sent the rest of the family home earlier to continue the preparations for the party that night at Dennis and Sharon's house. I was in shock but nonetheless sure that Christer would recover – telling me wonderful stories of what he saw during his near-death experience.

It was such a blessing to have my whole family together offering their love and support – parents, three brothers, three sisters-in-law, seven nephews, one niece, two aunts and three uncles. It was rare we were all together. What happened with Christer seemed to bring out all of our best selves. The small things that sometimes irritate us about each other fell away, letting love flow freely and abundantly.

That night I went back to the hotel to contact Christer's family in Sweden. I spoke with his three adult daughters and his brother asking them to contact Christer's mom who doesn't speak much English. Christer was due to visit them all in August. I told them we would know more after the hyperthermia treatment ended. I would be permitted to see him again on Monday morning when they would remove all sedation to see if he would regain consciousness. I prayed he would wake up and be his normal cheery self.

Sunday my family had brunch together and most of them began the journey back to their homes. I moved to Dennis' house where my parents were staying a few more days. That night Christer and I were supposed to see an old friend of mine from high school. Our 40th high school reunion was earlier in June. I didn't attend the reunion in suburban NY but many from my class of 99 girls had reestablished contact through an email list and a Facebook Group. Eleanor had gotten in touch with me because she was going through a life transition and was interested in learning more about our center in Peru.

When I called to tell her what happened to Christer, I learned she lived five minutes from the Palm Beach Gardens hospital where Christer was. We met for lunch between visiting hours to catch up on four decades. Fate had brought us together again under strange circumstances yet it was so comforting to be with someone who knew me so long ago and was so interested in my journey and my life in Peru. Like me, she had recently married after many years being single.

I arrived at the hospital Monday morning optimistic and hopeful. I had visualized Christer awake and alert but he was still unconscious. They had brought Christer's temperature back to normal but he was still sedated. His kidney and liver functions were low and his respiration was not stable so they didn't want to risk waking him. I sat by his side for three hours holding his hand. He had five doctors on his case – heart, lung, kidney, brain and primary care. The biggest concern of everyone was his brain function.

By Monday I had decided to put short updates of Christer's condition on Facebook in addition to emailing my family, our staff, friends and his family in Sweden. There was such an outpouring of love, prayers and energetic healing passing through the airwaves. I told Christer about all the responses we were getting. I trusted he could hear me and he would come back when he was able.

My shock and disbelief transformed into a super-present and conscious state. The mundane things of everyday life that often stress and annoy me disappeared. Human care and concern was what mattered most and it seemed to be everywhere around me. The nurses in the ICU were especially kind and helpful. They patiently taught me what all the numbers on the machines meant and how to look for positive signs.

Each doctor would make one brief visit a day. I listened carefully to what they had to say but something else was also going on in and around me. Christer and I had spoken many times about other forms of life and levels of existence. I knew well Christer would not want to be kept alive by machines. I also knew there were decisions that needed to be made on a soul level that would not necessarily be limited by the condition of his body. It was important for me to know where he was on that level and what he wanted to do.

On Tuesday, four days after he was admitted, his organs had stabilized enough to remove his sedation to see if he would wake up. His eyes opened for brief periods. He recognized my voice and could respond to my questions by blinking his eyes. He was still breathing on the respirator but his blood pressure and other organ functions were improving.

The EEG they did to test his brain waves, didn't reveal very much – low activity but no seizures. He seemed to me to be back in his body. He could move his legs a little but not his hands or arms. His face was responsive and expressive, even with his eyes closed. He knew his name and when I asked him to look at me and open his eyes, he responded to that request as best he could, but seemed to understand me. So I remained hopeful. I felt he wanted to live and was working hard to come back.

The next day was the first time I began to consider he might not recover. He was less responsive than he had been the day before. He opened his eyes briefly when I arrived but not after that. His pressure, heart beat and respiration were stable and the kidney and liver functions were improving slightly but all the doctors were concerned that he still wasn't awake, that his brain was damaged. The neurologist had said from the beginning that he likes to see the patient wake up within seven days. After that the likelihood of recovery is rare. I asked all the family and friends getting the daily reports from me to keep sending love and light, to visualize him awake and alert.

That night I wrote five psychic healer friends in various corners of the world and asked them to contact Christer at a soul level to get a sense about his brain and what he wanted to do, or was able to do. In a few more days, I would be asked to make a decision about his breathing tube and I wanted more than medical opinion.

My friend Yukia in South Africa, who stayed with us at Paz y Luz for several months, wrote me back first.

> *Dear sister,*
> *As a planetary being you know that the universe and our destinies are not always centered to our micro missions on earth. In the final decision he has to make, it surely*

plays a very crucial role, especially the love Christer has for you. He needs more time to decide what is more important for the highest good of our Earth. He has a very important role as the engineer of the new energetic magnetic Light in Sirius to be sent for the transition.

It is a momentous time for the Pleiadians and for his planet and we are just about to cross the white bridge of unconditional love to activate the doorways of full acceptance and surrender but we still have much opposition from others with distorted interests in our beautiful planet. We are all sending a lot of love to you and whatever the outcome is nobody else's to choose but Christer's!

I have been told this with utmost certainty even if he chooses to stay under critical circumstances. Like my Guide ascended Master Adamus tells me, "All is good in Creation and we just open our hearts to all potentials in full acceptance." I am sure that this is exactly what you are doing. Stay aware of all it could be, centered in Love. Give him time. I am with you daily to give you strength and courage.

Then I received this from Monse in Argentina:

I see him departing in a tube of light saying , "My moment has come. Only up to here I can accompany you. Don't cry for the love, it filled my soul. I depart content. I know your work is great, and what is coming is a very big test, and I also know it is a part of your living. I will be by your side forever. Allow my chest to stop. I feel so much love that I no longer can hold it. I feel so much love; give me your hand and hold it till I depart. I feel so much love. The door is already open."

In addition to those two messages, three other well trusted friends said he was asking for more time to decide. One said he was 50–50, which made it possible for me to believe both Yukia and Monse. In total, four people said he needed more time to decide. Karin is a spiritual friend from Sweden who also happens to be a neurologist. In her meditation she saw Christer one week in the future walking and talking normally. This surprised her from a clinical viewpoint but not from a spiritual perspective.

She wrote:

> *He said he wanted to live because of his children and you, and that his work here was not finished. He received some healing from the angels as I watched and after awhile we parted. I then moved ahead one week to the date July 1st to see if there was any change. Christer came and was the same as before.*

Two other friends, one in Peru and one in London, said to give him one more week to make his decision.

That day was very difficult for me but after hearing from my friends and having an intuitive sense that in fact he was being pulled in both directions, I felt calmer. When I was with him in the hospital, I could feel that pull within him. I wanted to give him whatever time he needed. I wanted to honor his decision whatever it might be. So I chose not to ask him directly to stay.

The next day things were more or less the same. He still wasn't awake but he opened his eyes a little longer than before. He had been off sedation for 24 hours. His legs and feet responded to pain stimulus but not his chest, arms or hands. I asked him three different questions that he directly responded to by blinking his eyes. When I asked him to turn his head, he made every effort to do so even though it didn't turn very much. I was encouraged he understood what I said.

The big medical question mark was still his brain and how much damage had been done to it. The other question for me was more important. What does he want to do – come back or move into the light?

On day seven, there wasn't much change. His daughters called on my cell phone which I held to his ear. It was clear he knew who they were. He responded to certain things they said by blinking his eyes. His expression was animated. I think it helped him to hear their voices speaking Swedish and feel their love through the airwaves.

Over the weekend there were substitute doctors so there were no important decisions to be made. I enjoyed the quiet time I had with Christer. I played his favorite music on my iPod with speakers, massaged his feet, held his hand. I spoke with him and read to him from a novel I had just started. I told him about all the people who were sending him love and light. I was conscious not to pressure him in any way to come back just for me.

Saturday, I decided to wear Christer's African shirt we bought in Johannesburg the previous year. He had a new nurse that day, who was from Zimbabwe. She asked me about the shirt and we had a lovely conversation. I told her I lived nine years in Johannesburg. She said Christer's kidney doctor, who I had met the day before, was from Johannesburg. As if on cue, the doctor walked in and we chatted about our days in Joburg. A little while later, the substitute lung doctor arrived, who was from Lima! We spoke like old friends as well. All these unusual connections somehow felt like a good sign.

Sunday morning, June 26, Christer was very tired and didn't open his eyes much or move at all. I told him his daughter Ulrika would be calling again soon at 11am. He opened his eyes and became more alert about five minutes before she called. While she was speaking to Christer, I asked him to blink his eyes if he could hear Ulrika, which he did.

I also asked him earlier if he could hear me and he blinked quite deliberately. That day was our third wedding anniversary. We had planned to celebrate on the beach in Jamaica but life doesn't always go the way we plan. Still, I felt blessed to be sitting by his side, holding his hand, grateful I was feeling love rather than anger or resentment. I was grateful to be fully present and open to what was happening around me. The love I felt was without condition – pure and unattached to outcome, which was quite beautiful.

I wondered what people do who don't believe in anything, who don't have a spiritual practice to support them at such crucial times. By being so present in the situation, I was able to see all the little things we normally miss in life – smiles, a gentle touch, a caring look, a song on the radio that sounds like an angel speaking directly to me. The whole experience felt like a special gift.

That night Yukia wrote me again with a new message. She said:

Christer is a guardian of the new magnetic light for the transition. He has a higher function and role than the one he has on earth. The inner conflict he has is between the unconditional love he feels for you and his mission in the realms. There are some negotiations taking place to rewrite his contract if he wishes, so that the potential of connecting the two might be co-created and his time extended. But his soul needs to be completely clear and right now his soul is tired and deep down wanting to go home. He asks for no interference and wants a field of stillness – a place in between where nothing exists but trust, love, compassion. He is asking for more time and he is sending his unconditional love to you.

Monday Christer was very tired, hardly opening his eyes. I trusted he was in a good place deciding what to do. I told him I loved him and wanted him to come back if he could. But if he needed to move on to the next level, I would help him do that. The decision was his and I would support him whatever he decided.

The neurologist reminded me we were past the seven-day marker. I asked him what he would do if Christer was his son. Without hesitation, he said he would remove the breathing tube. After he left the room, the song that came on my iPod was a medley by Barbara Streisand – *I Believe* and *You'll Never Walk Alone*.

For those of you who don't know these songs…

I believe for every drop of rain that falls,
A flower grows...

(... the second half of the song continues)

I believe above the storm, the smallest prayer
Will still be heard
I believe someone in the great somewhere
Hears every word
Every time I hear a newborn baby cry, or touch a leaf
or see the sky
Then I know why, I believe.

The second song is:

When you walk through a storm, hold your head up
high and don't be afraid of the dark.
At the end of the storm is a golden sky and the sweet
silver song of a lark.
Walk on through the wind, walk on through the rain
though your dreams be tossed and blown.
Walk on, walk on with hope in your heart and you'll
never walk alone. You'll never walk alone.

Tears came to my eyes at this beautiful reminder to keep believing no matter how things appear and to remember I am not alone, we are not alone. I knew there were forces bigger than all of us, assisting me and all the people who loved Christer, during this difficult time – no matter whether Christer came back to us or not.

Tuesday morning the lung doctor insisted we make some decision by the next day about Christer's breathing tube, which was put in by paramedics in the ambulance eleven days before. That type of tube should have already been replaced or removed. A possible alternative was to do a tracheotomy – a surgical procedure cutting a hole in his throat where a new ventilation tube would be inserted. The doctor said there was no reason "to put him through that" if we planned to transfer him to hospice care after Friday.

I didn't want to do the operation but I also wanted to make sure Christer and his daughters had enough time to feel comfortable with transferring him to hospice. The hospital staff had already told me about the hospice program based at the hospital. That day I went to see the facilities and spoke to Luanne who was extremely kind and caring. I was comfortable with the idea of moving him there, confident if he was still able to come back he could do it more easily from the beautiful hospice environment than from the ICU filled with blinking machines.

Christer seemed very far away. I called his name and he opened his eyes. "Christer honey, we have to make a decision about your breathing tube. Would you like me to remove it?" He blinked his eyes. "If you understand what I am saying, blink your eyes twice." He did. "I want to make sure I understand you well. Do you want me to remove the tube?" He blinked his eyes quite emphatically. "OK darling. We will do that. I love you."

That day was the most difficult for me. I came home and wrote to Christer's family explaining to them about the tracheotomy and the option of hospice care. My good friend Val, the storyteller who was present for the Gathering in 2008 where Christer dreamed United Vision into being, called me to offer her presence if I needed her. While discussing the idea with Sharon, my sister-in-law, I told her about my Once-Upon-A-Time story from that Gathering which Val had presented at our wedding.

I longed for my closest friends to be around me, to help create a special ceremony to assist Christer's spirit to leave his body. But they were far away and time was short. Sharon felt I was excluding her, which wasn't exactly true but I knew I had closed my heart in a way I hadn't since Christer entered the hospital. I wanted things to be different than they were.

The Andean Tradition has taught me to believe wherever we find ourselves at significant times, we have everything around us we need. On one level I knew that, but emotionally I had left the sacred space of the present moment and had projected myself into past comforts and an unmanageable future.

I went to bed early, exhausted from the day and slept for a few hours. At one a.m. I was wide awake running plans through my head, conversing with Sharon (who was asleep in her room) about our disagreement. Recognizing I would have to plan the ceremony myself, I thought about my Once-Upon-A-Time story and wondered if it could work as part of the ceremony. About 3 a.m. it was clear I wasn't going to fall back asleep so I got up to find the story in my computer.

I opened the document of our wedding ceremony. Not only did the story seem appropriate but the whole wedding ceremony seemed to be perfect down to the vows I made to him three years before.

I checked my email to find a letter from Ulrika, Christer's oldest daughter, saying the whole family agreed Christer's tube should be removed. She wrote: "Maybe he is needed somewhere else to continue his work with the Transition. Anyway, he's a free spirit and he needs his wings!"

That email and "finding" the right ceremony helped to re-open my heart. Everything I needed was indeed right there with me. I felt love pouring in and through me. It once again amazed me how different things feel with an open heart when in fact the circumstances are exactly the same as before. When our hearts are closed, everything is a struggle. When my heart opened, I felt so much support. I felt centered and calm; ready to assist Christer to pass peacefully.

There was another email from Monse in Argentina, quoting her message from Christer:

> *"I am very far away, my departure is imminent, she knows it… My relationship with Diane goes beyond the carnal, the love we share goes further than the distance that is apparent today. Her love, my love is only one. I am departing; there is only a thread between my body and me."*

Karin, Yukia and my other friends also shared with me Christer had made his decision. He was ready to move into the Light. Sharon and Dennis were up by 6:00 a.m... I asked Dennis to print out four copies of the ceremony. Before I could apologize to Sharon we hugged each other, eyes filling with tears, hearts open. No words necessary. She and Dennis would be with me for the ceremony. A few hours later I called Eleanor, my high school friend, to invite her to be part of the ceremony if she felt comfortable doing so. She was honored and agreed.

We called Hospice and they said they could take over the case at 2:00 p.m. that day. Their doctor would remove Christer's breathing tube. Sharon helped me organize what we wanted to bring. There is a beautiful version of Barbara Streisand singing *Somewhere* from West Side Story that we played at our wedding. We tried to find it on the internet but with no luck. We saw online a Barnes & Noble store near the hospital had a copy so we planned to go there after visiting Christer at 10 a.m.

All the connections that morning seemed grace-filled, like the Starkeepers were assisting us. When we got to B&N we were disappointed to learn they didn't have the Streisand album we wanted but we saw a display of a Jackie Evancho CD called *Dream with Me*. Sharon recognized her as the young singer Dennis had been so impressed with when he saw her on television. When I looked at the list of songs on *Dream with Me*, I was delighted to see track number seven was *Somewhere* from West Side Story, a duet with Barbara Streisand!

While I was signing papers with the hospital, Sharon was buying battery-lit scented candles for Christer's new Hospice room upstairs in the same hospital. Luanne had requested a music therapist to be present as they prepared to remove Christer's breathing tube. She sang his favorite songs slowly and gently as she played her guitar. It was very soothing for all of us. Even though we were still in the ICU room, the energy had totally changed once the hospice staff had taken over.

As the tube was removed, the therapist sang to the rhythm of Christer's breathing, to assist the transition for him to breathe without the machine. When he was breathing on his own and stable enough, he was moved upstairs to a lovely hospice room where we could be with him to perform the ceremony to release his spirit from his body. It was very peaceful and beautiful – such kind and caring people ministering to him.

Dream With Me was playing quietly as we set out the candles, crystals and a framed photo of Christer and me taken on our wedding day. Dennis, Sharon, Eleanor and I stood around Christer. As we were ready to begin, the sixth song on the album ended, as if on cue and *Somewhere* began playing.

> *There's a place for us,*
> *Somewhere a place for us.*
> *Peace and quiet and open air*
> *Wait for us*
> *Somewhere.*
> *There's a time for us,*
> *Some day a time for us,*
> *Time together with time spare,*
> *Time to learn, time to care,*
> *Some day,*
> *Somewhere.*
> *We'll find a new way of living,*
> *We'll find a way of forgiving*
> *Somewhere . . .*
> *There's a place for us,*
> *A time and place for us.*
> *Hold my hand and we're halfway there.*
> *Hold my hand and I'll take you there*
> *Somehow,*
> *Some day,*
> *Somewhere.*

Then Eleanor read a version of the Lord's Prayer I was told is a translation of the original Aramaic:

O cosmic birther of all radiance and vibration!
Soften the ground of our being and carve out a space within us where your presence can abide and your love and light shine forever.
Fill us with your creativity so that we may be empowered to bear the fruit of your mission.
Endow us with the wisdom to produce and share what each being needs to grow and flourish.
Let each of our actions bear fruit in accordance with our desire.
Untie the tangled threads of destiny that bind us, as we release others from the entanglements of past mistakes.
Do not let us be seduced by that which would divert us from our true purpose, but illuminate the opportunities of the present moment.
For you are the ground and the fruitful vision, the birthpower and fulfillment, as everything and everyone is gathered and made whole again.

Sharon then read the story I wrote in April 2008 during our Gathering to Envision, Experience and Manifest the world the way we want it to be:

Once upon a time there was a man and a woman who lived on Earth in different corners of the world. Before they came to Earth, they lived on the same star where they made a contract to meet when they knew the moment was right on Earth to change the world.
Many years passed on Earth and they experienced so much life they nearly forgot their promise. But one day,

*while the man and the woman were sleeping in their own
corners of the world, the Star-Giver blessed them with a
Star-kiss that helped them remember their soul contract.*

*In his dream the man saw a beacon of light from
the high Andes Mountains in Peru. He packed his bags
and journeyed to a small town along the river in the
Sacred Valley not knowing the woman would be there.
But because she too had been kissed by the Star-Giver, she
remembered her promise and was awaiting his arrival.
When they saw each other, their hands touched and their
hearts remembered everything.*

*Because the man and the woman had learned how
to come together in the balanced union of Love and Light,
they reflected the perfect union of male and female in the
divine creator. They were able to experience heaven on
earth and they lived happily ever after.*

Dennis then read one of my favorite Hafiz poems:

> *This place where you are right now*
> *This place where you are right now*
> *God circled on a map for you.*
> *Wherever your eyes and arms and heart can stretch*
> *Against the earth and sky*
> *The beloved has bowed there.*
> *Our beloved has bowed there*
> *Knowing you were coming.*

I then read my wedding vows to Christer:

> *I, Diane, chose you, Christer to be my husband,*
> *to love and give you my respect,*
> *to keep you in sickness and in health,*
> *to share my life openly with you,*

to speak truthfully and lovingly with you,
to accept you fully as you are
and delight in who you are becoming,
to respect your uniqueness,
encourage your fulfillment,
and compassionately support you
through all the changes of our years together,
so long as love and life shall endure.

And even beyond...

We closed with me reading the note that Christer's oldest grandson Anton sent me on behalf of his brothers and I added many other names:

Grandpa, we miss you a lot and love you so much. Right now we are at the Åland Islands, swimming, fishing, having a BBQ. We wish that you were here. Our thoughts are with you and we hope for the best. Right now we don't know so much about your future, we want you to know that we have a very very strong love for you. We want you to watch over us and support us in the future. You have to promise. Many many many kisses and hugs from your grandsons Anton, Simon and Adam, Johannes, Elias, and your daughters Josefin, Jessica, Ulrika, your mother Aina, your brother Anders, your sister Helena, your friend Bjorn, all of my family, the Paz y Luz family and all the people around the world that know you and love you.

We then stood by him, two on each side of the bed, visualized his spirit/soul and gently lifted it out of his physical body and sent it up to the heavens. The angelic music of *Dream With Me* continued to play as we talked quietly. I held Christer's warm hand and watched him breathe. When the last song finished playing for the second time, Christer exhaled. Then he was gone.

I feel blessed I was able to help him pass in a peaceful loving way, just as I promised him. Love is an incredible gift because it continues even after the one who taught you how to do it, passes on to the other side.

I feel even more connected with the Starkeepers since Christer's unexpected passing. Perhaps Christer was always a Star Being sent to me when back in 2007, I asked Spirit to bring the appropriate man to my door if I needed a relationship to heal my heart. He accomplished his mission and now he has returned to continue his work with the Starkeepers.

CHAPTER SEVENTEEN

CREATOR

the ninth rite

The Creator Rite, the second of the Rites to Come, connects you to the light within yourself – the Divine Source within – so you can co-create your life. When you receive this initiation, you awaken this God-light within you and acquire stewardship for all of creation. It awakens your God-nature and brings the cellular realization that Spirit is not only acting through you, but *is* you.

Although in the past, there were individuals who attained this level of initiation, and awakened their Christ or Buddha consciousness, it was not possible to transmit this from one person to another. So while Spirit-to-human transmission happened on occasion, human-to-human transmission only became possible recently.

The Creator Rite was brought forth in June of 2006 when The Four Winds Society organized two simultaneous sacred journeys to the two most powerful apus in southern Peru: Ausangate and Salkantay. Both groups included foreigners and indigenous mountain people from the Andes. Their mission was to do ceremony together which offered and asked for healing and forgiveness for all the atrocities committed against humanity and nature over time, in order to heal the planet and bring the Creator-energy back down to the people.

As they weathered the elements of snow and wind and sun, they journeyed deep inside themselves and with each other, touching old wounds, offering and receiving forgiveness, they healed old destructive patterns that had perpetuated the separation of humanity by race, culture and social status. By changing those patterns in ceremonies on the sacred mountaintops, they were able to bring back to us, the Creator-energy of the time to come. With this rite, we can co-create our life the way we want it to be.

I believe there is a force within each of us that longs for expansion, to know and experience new and better things beyond our current awareness. I think this urge was built into our program when human beings were created. You could even call it the spark of life within us – the fire, the inner creative force that activates this impulse. The Creator Rite ignites that spark, awakens that creative wisdom, so it can rise to its potential.

Perhaps you have felt that urge in your own life. Maybe it starts as dissatisfaction with the status quo, a discomfort for life as it is. It can also feel like something is calling you, calling you out of your complacency, like an inner voice saying, "Isn't there something more, something better?" When we recognize we can co-create our lives rather than wait for life to happen, then a new energy source is unleashed and we begin to see life differently.

One of the reasons I teach the Munay-Ki in conjunction with practices to connect with the four elements is because it links us with this unseen creative force. When we lie down on Pachamama and give her all our heavy energy – the heavy emotions that keep us trapped in our stories – she uses it like fertilizer and transforms it into new growth and new life. The Water soothes and balances us. The Air purifies and enlightens us, helping us to expand our consciousness, to see things from a broader perspective. The Fire transmutes our anger into passion and compassion; it changes coal into diamonds.

Two weeks after Christer's passing, I was back in Pisac teaching the Munay-Ki to a lovely small group from Texas and Argentina. They all knew about what had happened, some of them following the daily hospital messages on Facebook. It was such a gift to re-enter my life at Paz y Luz in this way: teaching the Munay-Ki and doing the exercises with the elements to help me transform all the heaviness into light.

When we can release the limitations of the past, we clear the way for a new refined energy to enter which helps us recognize we are co-creators, not pawns or victims. We may not be able to choose all the events we encounter in life but we can choose how we want to respond to them. That's how we transform difficult situations into opportunities and gifts.

I have a friend Emily, who has written a book called *Cancer Healed Me*. When she found out she had breast cancer five years ago, she decided not to treat it using the traditional medical model. Instead she pursued several alternative options which have enhanced her life in many wonderful ways.

I wondered after my own experience with Christer, if I was deluding myself in some way because I wasn't feeling devastated or depressed. But the more I look into myself and discuss the subject with others, I realize challenging, painful, sad, difficult events have as much (or maybe more) potential for creative expansion as do the events of our "normal" everyday life.

Exploring this idea, I asked myself what were the prerequisites enabling us to respond differently from the expected norm? While Christer was in the hospital, I was not aware of consciously choosing to stay open-hearted and present. So I presume it happened because some part of me was already pre-programmed by my spiritual practice and the magic Munay-Ki energy. However, I was aware the one day when my heart closed down, because it made my experience so much more difficult until I was able to open it again.

It was my belief for a long time that death is a natural part of our existence. It is sad for the people left behind to no longer have the physical presence of the one they loved. But for the person going, it is a transition to another plane of existence more beautiful than the one they are leaving behind. This was my belief.

But that belief had never been tested by reality. No one close to me had ever died (except my 99-year-old grandmother). I thought that test would come with one of my parents. I certainly didn't think it would be Christer. I met my soul mate when I was 54 – how could he be gone a mere four years later? That should be tragic, right?

Well, you could look at it that way of course but the surprising part for me was that I didn't experience it that way, then or now. Perhaps I had done enough healing of my inner wounds that I was able to be present to the situation without feeling sorry for myself. Remarkably, I didn't feel angry at Christer or God. I wasn't resentful, even on that day we should have been flying to Jamaica. I didn't feel abandoned or betrayed. I was sad but very grateful for all the support and kindness around me.

It was an indication for me, of the deep healing that took place within me during my relationship with Christer which also happened to be the period I first received the Munay-Ki Rites and began teaching them to others.

In a meditation recently, I asked Christer to tell me about soul-mates. He said:

> *Soul-mates are people who have soul contracts with each other. They made those contracts on a soul level before they were born – agreements to be fulfilled during their lifetime. Some of us have many soul contracts and some just a few. You and I had many contracts which is why we met late in our lives because we had other contracts to complete before we met. You had more contracts than I did and you still have some to go.*

He continued,

> *The soul connection you and I have is through many life times. We have a deep and primary connection that is still in place even though I am here and you are there. We still have agreements with each other to fulfill. The older the soul, the more contracts there are. You and I are very old souls.*
>
> *Not all soul contracts are romantic in nature. Some are even quite difficult. So "soul-mate" as most people understand the term isn't really about one's ideal romantic partner. We each have as many soul-mates as the soul contracts we made before we came into this life. You're my soul-mate, honey. No doubt about that.*

Maybe the deepness of the soul connection I feel with Christer is what made it possible for me to be so present with him in the hospital and help him pass over. I don't know. But the experience with Christer in the hospital definitely shifted something in my consciousness that now allows me to focus on human warmth and connection more than the stressful practicalities of daily life that before seemed so important. Of course there are certain business things that need attention but they don't require as much emotional investment as they did before.

So, in many ways I am better than I used to be, which I find extraordinary. I would have much preferred that Christer was still with me and we were living our special life together. But since that's not what happened, I am glad to have some unexpected benefits assisting me through this transition.

An Albert Einstein quote I saw on the internet said, "Everything is energy and that's all there is to it. Match the frequency of the reality you want and you cannot help but get that reality. It can be no other way. This is not philosophy. This is physics." He calls it physics. I call it magic. Either way, it is quite possible for any of us to do: energetically match the frequency of the reality we want – this is the magic of the Munay-Ki.

So, what are some of the prerequisites?

Heal your wounds, release your shit.

I mentioned before Pachamama receives all our heavy energy like a gift because for her, it is fertilizer that she needs in order to make things grow, to nourish and sustain us and all life. This exchange is the created way of things, the law of nature. So it is with our created selves: we eat and drink to sustain ourselves. The body uses what it needs and eliminates the rest. If we don't eliminate the waste, the body doesn't function well. It gets clogged and the systems start to break down.

It is the same with our emotional, spiritual and psychic bodies. We need to release things we no longer need, that no longer serve us. When we clear out the blocks, the energy can flow freely and we can respond in healthy ways to whatever circumstances we encounter, to create a grace-filled experience.

I had a friend in South Africa who was an anti-apartheid activist for 30 years. He spent six years on Robben Island in the '60s. In 1977 he was detained by the authorities and tortured nearly to death. When Joe felt he was dying, he called on a God he hadn't believed in since his childhood, to take his soul. At that moment he heard an inner voice tell him, "I have given you life and they will not take it away." Then the torture stopped. He told me an extraordinary story of how he then became friends with one of his guards. When he was eventually released, he began working with the Justice and Reconciliation department of the South Africa Council of Churches. He said to me, when we met in 1990, "Our God is a foolish God who asks us to do foolish things, like love our enemies."

I doubt Emily wanted to get cancer or Joe wanted to be detained and tortured. It is not the circumstances themselves I am suggesting are welcome events, anymore than I wanted Christer to have a pulmonary embolism that caused his death. But the most liberating beautiful truth we can know is despite whatever challenging circumstance we may find ourselves in, we can use our co-creative abilities to turn it into something growth filled and powerful.

Open your heart.

I learned the importance of keeping my heart open during my relationship with Christer. That argument we had before our Releasing Fear workshop highlighted for me that all things are possible with an open heart and conversely, when one's heart is closed, those possibilities are hidden behind locked doors. Akiyah gave Christer and me the key to our locked door when he asked us to remember the love we had for each other. He invited us to tune into that love and put aside our differences.

Holding hands with our eyes closed, I became aware I couldn't feel the love. It was only then I recognized my heart was closed. It no longer was a matter of solving the problem between us. The dilemma shifted from outside circumstances to inside me. How could I reach the love I knew was there? How could I free myself from my self-created prison? What did Einstein say? "Match the frequency of the reality you want and you cannot help but get that reality."

When Christer reached out to me, the prison door flung open and so did my heart. Love poured out of it and into it. Everything that before seemed broken and irreparable, melted away. With our connection to one another restored, we were able to prepare for the workshop in a matter of minutes. In an outward sense, the circumstances causing our problem had not changed but the situation between us had changed completely, thereby resolving the problem.

The flat tire incident a year later was easier for me to handle because by then I was able to look inside myself to work on my own blocks. Even though that long day with Christer in the car was challenging, I knew I couldn't open Christer's heart for him. I might have tried a few times, but mostly I was focused on what was going on with me and how to take care of myself without closing my heart to Christer.

The day of our workshop, Christer reached out to me. The morning after our flat tires, I was able to reach out to him. But in both cases, it was because something inside each of us had shifted. In the hospital, faced with the unthinkable, my heart stayed open by default rather than conscious choice. It made dealing with the events of those twelve days so much easier. Now, when it really mattered, my heart knew what to do.

Accept what is.

There is a very fine line between accepting reality as it is and creating the reality you want. Emily had breast cancer; Joe was a prisoner; Christer was in a coma in the ICU. It was important that each of us accepted those realities before we could begin to create our conscious responses to those circumstances. Acceptance is about being in the present moment. It means we acknowledge our limits. Acceptance is actually a form of liberation; it is a letting go, a pause, a release.

Accepting Christer was in critical condition permitted me to be fully present with him, which was an amazing gift. Wanting something to be different than it is, is not what creates a new reality. First we have to accept what is, then use our creative abilities to make of that circumstance an opportunity for growth. Wanting something to be different than it is, takes us out of the present moment, which is the only place that we can create anything. Having a clear intention for what we want to create is important, but releasing that intention into the creative field is a necessary part of manifesting it. Letting it go gives us the ability to stay in the present.

The hardest day I had in the hospital was the day I resisted the reality that Christer was choosing to go. It was the day I closed off to my sister in law and wanted my far-away friends to be there instead. The day we moved Christer to hospice and did the ceremony helping him to pass over, was beautiful and grace-filled because I accepted what was happening and opened myself to experience it fully.

Heidi, one of my Munay-Ki students in 2009, sent me this beautiful poem. Heidi's husband of 30 years, Carlos, died a few months before Christer. These words came to her daughter Simone just before Carlos died. She prayed and asked in desperation, "How can I go on living without my dad?" Here is what the universe sent her at that moment. She could barely write it down fast enough:

> *Happiness is not a goal or something we search for, it is an instinct we have in our earthly bodies, one that reminds us of our glory in Heaven. We do not have to search outside of ourselves to feel this peace again, we need only to love, to love unconditionally and then we will remember what heaven is. Even if you feel you have lost everyone and everything, love yourself and you will have lost nothing and you will have the world to gain.*
>
> *When you find yourself having begrudging thoughts,*

love instead. Love will feed you the strength you need.
Send it and you will receive it.

That is all we need to do – is to love

To find love in places of pain, to persevere with it
beside us and let it always guide us back to the beginning.
When the truth is heard, it will resonate with your soul in
a way that moves you from one state of being to another.

As I write this, it has been almost four months since Christer passed. I still miss him in physical form but I continue to feel his presence around me in sweet and funny ways. I have a special childhood friend named Terry. We've seen each other only a few times since my dad was transferred from Cincinnati to New York when I was twelve. But Terry and I have written to each other these past 40-some years on a regular basis. She has a collection of post cards I have sent her from all my travels. As always, this past September she sent me a birthday package which I waited until my actual birthday to open.

The morning of my birthday (which I had planned to spend with Christer in Amsterdam), I was home soaking in my bath and talking with Christer on the other side. I said to him, "You have to give me a present today so I know you are there. It has to be something that I will know is from you".

When I opened Terry's card later, I was looking at all the enclosures. I saw a copy of the post card I sent her from Sweden in August, when I was there to spread Christer's ashes with his family. Amazingly, the photo on the card was taken by a photographer named Christer Lundin, which I hadn't noticed when I bought the post card! In Terry's package, there was another post card entitled "Spirit". It was an abstract painting with a figure in white, floating at the top reaching down to what appeared to be mountains. The figure looked remarkably like Christer.

Then I read Terry's story about the shiny nickel she had enclosed in the packet. She found it in the sand the day after Christer passed, where she was doing a good-bye ceremony for him by the Lake near her home. She sent it to me for my birthday saying "Hope Christer's presence is with you on your birthday".

Did I co-create that delightful birthday present from Christer? Did Terry? Did he? In any case, co-creation can be magical. Christer had a great fascination for life in different dimensions so I am sure from where he is, he continues to co-create United Vision and to assist us with the big change that's coming. I look forward to expanding my consciousness more to work with him on that level, even though we are now in different dimensions.

There are times when I feel sad and lonely. I remember, back in the early '90s living in South Africa, my friend Joe used to tell me to "count your blessings" when I was feeling bad. At the time I rejected the idea thinking he was suggesting I deny or cover up my feelings. I thought expressing my feelings was a healthier way to be. What I know now that I didn't then is there is a difference between reacting to our feelings and being consciously aware of our feelings.

For example, just because we feel angry about something doesn't mean we have to scream and shout to express that anger, which actually keeps us in an angry state. On the other hand, it is important to be conscious that we are feeling or holding anger, which is toxic to our system. So pushing it down and not letting it out, is not a good idea either. Rather, we can release that anger by giving it to Pachamama or let some flowing Water wash it away. We can breathe deeply, with our eyes closed in a relaxed state to let it go, release it. Or we can count our blessings; see the glass half full instead of half empty. We can shift our consciousness from what we are feeling, toward what we want to be feeling. But it does involve conscious awareness. It is a process. The Munay-Ki Rites assist us with that process.

Five weeks after Christer passed, I traveled to Sweden to bring some of his ashes to his family. His three daughters organized a very moving memorial service in a small rustic chapel on the edge of a forest. Inside that womb-like space, I cried more than I had since the days in the hospital. Surrounded by Christer's five beautiful grandsons and daughters, his mother and the rest of the family, I sobbed and sobbed – for my loss, for their loss, for the unexpected turn of events that bound us so tightly together. The love flowed as powerfully as our tears, allowing us to feel a deep supportive connection with each other, Christer's spirit and Divine Source.

My feelings of sadness ebb and flow. I remember the process and keep working on the prerequisites. I went to Cusco the other day to buy supplies for Paz y Luz and take care of other business. Christer and I used to go together once a week. That day I asked Christer's spirit to be with me. In the physical he was a big strong guy who always carried the heavy supplies. Rather than bemoaning his absence, I called on his spirit for assistance. A station wagon taxi pulled up just as I exited the store, overloaded with packages. I was about to get in when a cute little boy opened the front door and hopped in. Before I could say anything, the driver smiled and said, "My son". He had stopped to pick up his son, not me, but he gladly took us both. I had to laugh as I thanked Christer.

On the way home, I was listening to a Carole King CD and was struck by the lyrics of the old '60s' song, *Up on the Roof*:

> *When this old world starts getting me down*
> *and people are just too much for me to face,*
> *I climb way up to the top of the stairs*
> *and all my cares just drift right into space.*
> *On the roof is the only place I know,*
> *where you just have to wish to make it so…*
> *At night the stars put on a show for free*
> *and you can share it all with me.*
> *Up on the roof, everything is alright."*

I wonder if Carole King and Gerry Goffin were aware of any spiritual metaphor when they wrote that song back in 1962. For me the words are a beautiful illustration of how important it is for us to go higher when every day realities seem to be limiting our creativity. It's important to let our cares drift into space, to see the beauty above and around us even when situations are difficult. These are the moments that can become our most valuable opportunities to ignite the God-Light within us; to co-create the world the way we want it to be.

CHAPTER EIGHTEEN

THE TIME IS NOW

When I moved to Peru in 2000, the Incan and Mayan prophecies about 2012 seemed a bit far in the distance. Now the time has arrived. We are inside the changes predicted more than 500 years ago. The prophecies are not so much about a specific day in a specific year but about a time. And the time is now.

While I have been writing this book, Egypt and Libya had people's uprisings. The Occupy Wall Street protests have spread around North America, Britain, Europe and Australia. It is as if people have just woken up from a long sleep to recognize their interests were not being served by the people in power – politically, economically and environmentally. Floods, tornadoes, volcanoes, tsunamis and droughts are happening with greater frequency and severity. The poles are shifting, the magnetic field is decreasing, and the ice caps are melting.

The change we have been waiting for is upon us. It means more than ever it is important for us to learn how to respond in a healthy positive way to the circumstances around us. It is time to expand our consciousness and amplify our awareness so we don't feel lost and confused. There are many beings and forces in the unseen world assisting us at this time. The energy transmissions from the Munay-Ki Rites act as codes to awaken our inner knowing. This is especially important when so much is shifting around us. The stability we seek at such a time can best be found inside ourselves and in our connection with the unseen world.

Silvia, my Peruvian friend who has lived in South Africa for 30 years, sent me a beautiful letter about the magic of the Munay-Ki at work in her life seven months after receiving the rites from Christer and me.

Dear Diane

It is time to put into words the magic of the Munay-Ki I am nurturing in my heart this year 2011. Even though I have been an initiate of the Andean Tradition since 2004, I was still struggling with some of the principles of the Tradition. In February, during the workshop with you and Christer, my frequency of vibration became attuned with the Nine Munay-Ki Rites, and I realized I had been handling those principles at an intellectual level. The Rites freed me to live the Tradition, not analyze it — for that I am deeply thankful to you and Christer.

Meeting Christer in Johannesburg just before the Munay-Ki workshop was beautiful, all smiles and simple words; and the most remarkable energy for me was to see and feel the perfect flow of munay (love) between your hearts! Receiving the rites from the two of you was just amazing; I knew the energetic seeds were going to start a natural, organic/spiritual process in me in preparation for reconnecting with my cosmic self. The weeks of work with the seven archetypes were awesome, and I had the opportunity to be in the balanced energy of the Munay-Ki when I needed it most.

Through my work as a conference interpreter I travel into Africa. I went to Ethiopia (Addis Ababa) once in January and twice in May. I always carry my mesa and do ceremony and energy work wherever I go. Ethiopia is a powerful place, so many ancient energies being guarded by the land, the people, and the gods. It is also the headquarters of the African Union, so I have the chance to ground light/love/harmony energies in the halls and corridors of the buildings as well as in the hearts of African heads of state and government.

I feel I have had lifetimes in that part of the African continent, my heart dances just being there; the people in Ethiopia are kind and loving, very tolerant of each other, half of the population is Christian and half Muslim. They treat each other with great respect, and even though the population is quite poor, one is able to see the dignity in their eyes. Ethiopia is one of the few African states never to be colonized. The people do not have in their collective history the experience of domination and oppression which is unique in this continent!

So by the time I completed my two-week energy integration with the Pachakuti archetype (of the Harmony Rite), I became aware of the interesting set of possibilities before me as I was hired to work in Addis for two different meetings, one for the African Union and the other for NGOs invited by the World Bank. I asked a close friend in the Andean community if she could channel a message for me before I went, which she did:

Beautiful One, I saw you as a staff that was put in the ground in the centre of everyone to hold the light and channel love, peace and harmony in ever widening circles. It is elucidation coming through to you from above. The Ark of the Covenant is in Ethiopia, it holds deeply sacred energy. So the image I saw was of a staff in the sacred heart of the land and you are the staff, the form through which the energy channels. You are the energy of radiating love. Let the energy of the Munay Ki flow.

Earthkeeper, Spirit says that you are meeting those that you have agreements with from the ethers, that all you need to do is hold your light powerfully. Remember each day to re-energize the Bands of Power. Your intuition will be working very powerfully; do not at anytime doubt yourself.

My next assignment into Africa was the African Union summit of heads of state and government in Equatorial Guinea, the only Spanish speaking country in Africa; this territory was colonized initially by the Portuguese and then overtaken by the Spanish while all surrounding territories were colonized by France and Belgium.

This area was exploited for wood, cacao, coffee, bananas, whatever agriculture was established by the Europeans – probably in the dark era of slavery, many atrocities were committed against this people too. One can still sense the deep suffering in the land and the hearts of the people. In 1968 Spain granted independence to Equatorial Guinea following the trend in the continent, leaving a puppet regime as France and Belgium had done, basically, a once off "democratic elections" exercise that in fact resulted in another dictator going mad in Africa.

So an army officer grabbed power in this forgotten little country and eventually in 1979 was ousted by his nephew who became president for life. The actual population remained uneducated, extremely poor and repressed by the tyrant in power.

At the turn of the century oil was found and suddenly this dictator became one of the wealthiest Africans in the continent. This attracted the business of the Americans (oil companies), the Chinese, the Europeans of course, the African 'powers' such as Egypt, Nigeria, South Africa, Morocco, also the Israelis and any company that could bring its services to this man and his family sitting on the biggest pile of money they could ever dream of.

The problem is that only the president and his family

benefit from the wealth of the country. The people remain unskilled and uneducated, also disempowered, mistrusting, despondent, sly, rude; absolutely the opposite to the Ethiopians!

I spent ten days in Equatorial Guinea, working for the African Union. Every morning I tried to do my Andean ceremony as in Ethiopia, to ground the energy of Love, Peace and Harmony in the continent. But connecting to Pachamama was extremely difficult; connecting to the hearts of the Equatorians was very hard. I needed help.

On July 1ˢᵗ 2011, the third day of Christer's transition, his luminous energy came to my side here in this hardened African land where the heads of state and government were meeting. I laid out my little mesa, was guided to make a heart with my rainbow ribbon from Cusco, had three coca leaves placed honoring the three worlds, had seven stones to be placed on each energy centre invoking the seven archetypes: serpent had a black stone from Lima, Puma had a white stone with a hole in the middle from the Dead Sea, Condor had a red stone from Urubamba river, Hummingbird had a heart shape rose quartz from South Africa, Huascar had a triangle shape lapis lazuli, Quetzacoatl had an arrow head shape kyanite crystal and Pachakuti had an oval shape white stone from Lacar lake in the Argentinean Patagonia.

Christer's energy enfolded me with his gentle but firm force and spoke the seven directions invocation in English (when I call the directions I normally do it in Quechua), and proceeded to bring and ground the energies of balanced munay, peace, tolerance, understanding, respect, harmony, light, love, healing and of course unity. His united vision was planted in this African soil; was received in joy by Pachamama, by MamaAfrica. Later that day, I worked at a closed session of the AU presidents dealing with the situation of civil war in Libya. I was able to hold this frequency vibration of unity and bring it to the hearts of each African leader in the room.

Diane, you had asked for a story of how the Munay-Ki had brought magic into our lives. Imagine Christer's United Vision already in motion here in Africa in 2011... Magic!

Many people who received the Munay-Ki have experienced big changes in their lives.

Brigitte, from Antwerp, Belgium writes:

The changes the Munay-Ki brought for me were not always comfortable but at the end of the dark tunnel only peace was waiting for me. The Munay-Ki has given me courage to feed my children and to make a home by myself. I stopped being a victim, a woman with no words, with no opinion. I became a woman of wisdom and power to stand on my two feet and to hold the Universe in my hands. I started to dream the world into being. I thank every Rite, every experience that is making my life into magic.

Munay means love in Quechua – munay-ki, I love you. So much has been said and written and produced about love. My dictionary says love is profound affection and deep devotion between persons. I would like to expand that definition beyond affection, devotion and desire. I think of Love as a frequency that opens our hearts so we can experience life with all its magic. It is the energy fuel that allows us to sing, laugh, play, smile, hope, create, transform and blossom. Love is a sensation, the essence of life itself. It is what makes our heart beat. Love is connection. It is what connects us heart to heart with others, nature and all creation.

Love is a vibration that both soothes and excites. It isn't something you "have" for someone else; it is a state of being that radiates out from the one who is in that state. It is contagious, that's why it feels like it is attached to another. When two people have a heart/soul connection, they are elevated to the love-frequency so that sensation is shared. But one or the other can pop themselves out of that frequency with any manner of stress and strain, fear or irritation. Between people with a heart/soul connection the love is always there and available but if one or the other opt into another frequency, it feels like they have lost the love.

That's what would sometimes happen with Christer and me, like before our Releasing Fear workshop or the day in South Africa with the flat tires. So how do we stay in the love frequency? The first thing we need to understand is this frequency is not exclusive to romantic lovers or family members. It is a frequency accessible to any of us at any time.

I was in that frequency during most of Christer's stay in the hospital. That open-heartedness I felt wasn't only for Christer but for his nurses and doctors and other hospital staff – even the woman who worked in the billing department. I felt it with my brothers and their wives and children. I felt it with the women who taught the yoga classes I attended and with my high school friend Eleanor; with the gas station attendant and the sales woman at Barnes and Noble. I was inside that frequency, so most of the time love wasn't directed at a person, it was simply the essence I floated in.

One of the reasons we like being around couples in love is because they exude the love frequency (more often than not) and it spills over on to us. But learning how to live in that frequency involves learning how to love ourselves and our lives in the moment. To love ourselves means we have to accept ourselves just as we are and delight in who we are becoming. That was my favorite of all our wedding vows which I would repeat often (to myself if not always to Christer): "I accept you fully as you are and delight in who you are becoming." It implies that even as we accept ourselves (very important step to accepting the other) we know there are possibilities for growth and development. They aren't mutually exclusive.

A friend and Munay-Ki student from the States, Cheryl[6], found out her husband John was having an affair with a woman he would see on his periodic business trips overseas. To make it even more complicated, Cheryl only discovered this news after her husband had died unexpectedly of a heart attack six months before. She found some love letters hidden in his papers.

She was very much in love with John and shocked that he could have been having an affair without her knowing it. She was still mourning his loss when she discovered the letters. Cheryl wondered how it could be possible that she had not noticed anything strange when he would return from these trips.

---

[6] For privacy reasons, some small details have been altered and the names have been changed to Cheryl, John and Anne.

Some days passed as she processed the news. She told me that the practices with the elements I had taught her were very helpful as was working with all the archetypes from the Harmony Rite. I suggested she also try talking with John on the other side, (in a meditative state with a written dialogue) as I had been doing with Christer. Maybe he would be able to help her understand both relationships better. When she wrote back to me, I asked her if I could share her story in this book and she agreed, if I would change their names.

This is the conversation Cheryl had with John:

Cheryl: *They say we are in a time where we need to release all the dark and hidden things… Maybe that is why it was necessary for me to find your love letters from Anne. What do you have to say about that?*

John: *Well firstly, I'm sorry. It was very difficult for me to deal with but it just happened – we met at a business conference. The connection felt very powerful.*

Cheryl: *So why did you continue here with me if you wanted to be with her?*

John: *I didn't want to be with her in that way. It was nice to be with her when I was away, but I was committed to you and my life here. I loved you. I never stopped loving you. It's good you found out. I was leading you there. It helps you to have a more complete view of me and not just an idealistic one. You are so much stronger than I was. It was always hard for me to choose, to be clear and strong. Like you are. That's why I was with you. Anne wasn't strong either.*

Cheryl: *OK, I want to understand this more. But I'm going to sleep now. We'll talk again in the morning or visit me in my dreams.*

John: *I love you*

Cheryl: *Yeah, sure.*

6:15 a.m. (next day)

Cheryl: *So, I didn't sleep much. Can you tell me more about how it was for you?*

John: *My darling Cheryl. I am so sorry that you are hurting. I didn't want that for you and I don't want that for you. When you work through this for yourself, you will have a deeper understanding about life and even love. For me, it wasn't about choosing between the two of you. The feelings I had for you and Anne were different. She needed me in a way that you didn't. What we (you and I) had together was solid and real and purposeful. With Anne it was like a fantasy — isolated moments in time.*

Cheryl: *Was your plan to just continue seeing her once a year, letting her believe that one day you'd be together?*

John: *I didn't really have a plan. She wanted more than I could give her yet when we were together, it was good. It felt like we fed each other in a way I didn't feel with you.*

Cheryl: *Why did you stay with me then?*

John: *Because I loved you and wanted to make a life with*

you. It's a good thing I died really, because it wasn't something I was handling very well. You both wanted more from me than I could give.

Cheryl: *John, I just can't work this out for myself — especially the lying part. I would have much preferred that you told me.*

John: *Well, I'm telling you now and still it is difficult for you.*

Cheryl: *Because it makes everything a lie!*

John: *No it doesn't. It makes both circumstances true. Dualities don't really exist. It is neither one nor the other extreme. It is somewhere in the more complex middle, that you need to make peace with.*

Cheryl: *My heart hurts. Literally, I feel pain on my left side of my chest. I just want to hate you and shut you out forever, even though I know that isn't the whole truth. I know our relationship was also full of beautiful moments that were very healing for both of us. I may as well keep on healing. My understanding of who you were doesn't fit with this current info so I'll have to redesign it in my mind and heart.*

The morning after that, I woke up angry, calling John a fucking, lying, cheating bastard, which I guess he was. But does that mean he wasn't also kind, caring, loving and supportive? Does that mean what we had together was invalid, not true, all a lie? How strange I never picked up anything that would indicate he was anything but happy with his life here with me. Maybe he was — happy with his

201

life here with me. I guess I will never know for sure.

I have been reviewing all the times in my life, before meeting John, when I participated in something similar and I do know from experience that you can love two people at the same time and have sexual experiences with both of them without negating the feelings for either one. But I wasn't as conscious then as I am now. I doubt I could be able to carry on a lie for two years without wanting to talk about it with the person to whom I had committed myself. I had no interest in other men, once I met John eight years ago. I thought I had found the love of my life.

I sent her the section I had written in the Creator chapter about receiving the challenges in our life as opportunities, hoping the same criteria could apply in this case, as with Emily's cancer, Joes' torture and Christer's passing: stay open hearted; forgive our human errors; accept what is and release anything that no longer serves us.

Some weeks later, she wrote me back to say thank you for helping her see the situation from a different perspective. She was able to move through her anger, forgiving her husband, herself and even the other woman. Cheryl told me she felt the presence of the luminous beings of the Healer Rite assisting her to heal.

Maybe the reality of John's relationship with Anne makes my relationship with him a fuller more complete love story than without it, especially because my relationship with John had always given me opportunities to heal my old issues regarding love and commitment. This has been another opportunity for me to go deeper into myself and my own understanding of the limitless possibilities of love. As he told me in our conversation, now I can see him in a fuller way and not just idealize him, which we tend to do when someone we love dies. I feel like I am ready to move on now in a way I couldn't before, so that is really a gift. I'm sure I still have more processing to do but I feel so much better now than I did when I first discovered those letters, and truthfully, I feel better now than I did before I discovered those letters. Thank you for all your support and advice. Thank you for the Munay-Ki.

I think it is important that we, humanity, learn more healthy ways to face the truth and try to step out of moral judgments to find a holistic, open, balanced way of being in the world. Love is complicated, complex. Relationships are full of contradictions because we are human beings who don't always make the best choices. We are evolving; we are healing; we can be the change we want to see in the world. We can learn to forgive the unforgivable. We can learn to embrace the challenges as the gifts they are. To accomplish this is to be free, whole, unlimited. Love, with all its complexity, is what really matters most. Life is truly interesting, just when you think you have it all figured out, it invites you to see more, go deeper, higher and broader.

A week or so before Christer and I flew up to Florida, Christer decided to make a giant heart out of river stones in one of our empty lots. He said his spirit guide told him to do it. I was busy writing this book so I didn't ask any questions and wasn't too happy with the interruption when he asked my help to outline the shape of the heart. It seemed so urgent and important to him. He picked the whitest stones from the river he could find and made three rows of stones side by side forming the heart. He placed a large quartz crystal in the center and put four white chairs back to back facing the four directions. He said people could meditate there and maybe it would become something else in the future. He wanted the heart to be visible from above so people could see it from the road that snakes down from Cusco into Pisac.

Knowing Christer, I'm sure he also hoped it would become a landing pad for his extraterrestrial friends to visit us more easily. Perhaps on some level, he knew he wasn't going to be back and wanted to create this reminder for me and others to remain big-hearted – to remember that he is my bridge and my guide, just as I was told on that ancient rock in Italy after the 2010 Munay-Ki workshop there.

When our staff and friends in Pisac heard Christer was in the hospital, his "heart" became the place people gathered to pray for him and send him healing. When I returned to Paz y Luz with Christer's ashes, we did the first of several memorial ceremonies inside that heart. Everyone got to sprinkle some of his ashes around the perimeter of the heart where we sat and then we buried some in the middle.

I know for him, that heart in the field meant Love in its biggest and broadest sense. He knew when we are vibrating in the frequency of Love, the magic of life abounds.

"Magic," he told me as I sat meditating in that heart this morning, "is delightful, stimulating, fun. Magic is something we utilize to create." The right hemisphere of the brain is our creative side, which isn't logical, practical or linear. It's rather the place where creative energy flows free from form or meaning which only later becomes a creation. When an artist creates a painting, she gathers brushes, colors, canvas, strings and other things. But magic is what takes those elements and tools and makes them into a creative work of art. Same as a bag full of words becomes sorted by the poet to make a poem.

Magic is going out of the literal material realm into the zone of image and sensation that follows the wind, looks behind the rainbow and lets the imagination soar. When we allow our consciousness to expand, then we can tap into the many resources that exist in other dimensions.

The Munay-Ki gives us access to those assistants in the other dimensions with formulas, codes, keys and vibrations. I believe the Munay-Ki is a gift from the Star Beings and it is spreading so quickly and widely because as many people as possible need to be prepared for the change that is upon us. The codes of the Munay-Ki Rites open people's awareness and expand their abilities to see things in creative loving ways.

Access the Magic. The time is now.

APPENDICES

APPENDIX A – The Nine Rites

The Nine Rites are broken up into three categories:
- Foundation Rites
- Lineage Rites
- Rites to Come

The Foundation Rites are:
1. Healer Rite
2. Bands of Power Rite
3. Harmony Rite
4. Seer Rite

The Lineage Rites are:
5. Daykeeper Rite
6. Wisdomkeeper Rite
7. Earthkeeper Rite

The Rites to Come are:
8. Starkeeper Rite
9. Creator Rite

1. HEALER RITE connects you to a lineage of shamans from the past who come and assist you in your personal healing, offering you tremendous spiritual assistance. These luminous beings work on you during your meditation and sleep time to heal the wounds of the past and of your ancestors.

2. BANDS OF POWER consist of five energetic bands representing earth, water, fire, air, and pure light. These bands are activated in your luminous energy field, and act as filters, breaking down into one of the five elements any heavy energy that comes your way so that this energy can feed you instead of making you toxic or ill. Once activated, the Bands of Power are always 'on'. In a world filled with fear, the bands provide essential protection.

3. HARMONY RITE plants seven archetypes into your chakras:

- In the first chakra, you receive the archetype of serpent.
- In the second chakra you receive the archetype of the jaguar/puma.
- In the third chakra you receive the archetype of the hummingbird
- In the fourth chakra you receive the archetype of the eagle/condor.

Then, three "guardians" go into your upper three chakras.

- In the fifth chakra you receive the archetype of Huascar, the keeper of the lower world, the unconscious.
- In the sixth chakra you receive the archetype of Quetzal-coatl, the feathered serpent, keeper of the middle world (our waking world)
- In the seventh chakra you receive the archetype of Pacha-kuti, the protector of the upper world (our super-conscious).

These archetypes are transmitted into your chakras as seeds. These seeds germinate with fire, and you have to perform a number of fire meditations to awaken them and help them grow. Afterward, they help transmute the psychic sludge that has built up in your light body, so your chakras can shine with their original light.

4. SEER RITE installs filaments of light extending from your visual cortex in the back of your head to your third eye and heart center. This installation awakens your ability to perceive the invisible world, to see and know with your heart and your intuition.

5. DAYKEEPER RITE is an energetic transmission that connects you to a lineage of shaman from the past. The Daykeepers were the masters of the ancient stone altars found in sacred places throughout the world, from Stonehenge to Machu Picchu. The Daykeeper is able to call on the power of these ancient altars to heal and bring balance to the world.

According to lore, the Daykeepers called on the sun to rise each morning and set each evening, made sure humans were in harmony with Mother Earth (Pachamama), and honored the ways of the feminine. The Daykeepers were the midwives who attended births and deaths, as well as being herbalists, and traditional healers. They were generally women, and were knowledgeable about the ways of the feminine earth. This initiation begins the process of healing your inner feminine, and helps you to step beyond fear and practice peace.

6. WISDOMKEEPER RITE helps you to step outside of time and taste infinity. The legends say the ancient wisdom resides in the high mountains. The ice-covered peaks were revered as places of power, just as other mountains around the world, from Mt. Sinai to Mt. Fuji to Mt. Olympus, have been honored as places where humans meet the divine. The lineage of Wisdomkeepers consists of medicine men and women from the past who defeated death and stepped outside of time.

7. EARTHKEEPER RITE connects you to a lineage of archangels that are guardians of our galaxy. They're reputed to have human form and to be as tall as trees. The Earthkeepers, who are stewards of all life on the Earth, come under the direct protection of these archangels and can summon their power when they need to in order to bring healing and balance to any situation. The Rite of the Earthkeeper helps you learn the ways of the seer, and to dream the world into being.

8. STARKEEPER RITE anchors you safely to the time after the great change that is said will occur around the year 2012. According to lore, when you receive this Rite, your physical body begins to evolve into that of "homo luminous". The aging process is slowed down, and you become resistant to diseases to which you were once vulnerable. After receiving this Rite, you may notice you no longer process events occurring in your life primarily at the physical level but rather, at the Spirit level. When you receive these Rites, you acquire stewardship of the time to come and for future generations.

9. CREATOR RITE connects you to the light within yourself – the Divine Source within – so you can co-create your life. It awakens your God-nature and brings the cellular realization that Spirit is not only acting through you, but *is* you, ineffable Pure Consciousness. This Rite was not available before 2006 on the planet. Although there were individuals who attained this level of initiation, and awakened their Christ or Buddha consciousness, it was not possible to transmit this Rite from one person to another, until now. www.munay-ki.org

APPENDIX B – Origins of the Munay-Ki

There has been a lot of discussion about the origins and authenticity of the Munay-Ki. I would like to express my feelings about "authenticity" in relation to the Andean spiritual tradition as well as the Munay-Ki.

The Andean spiritual tradition is not an organization. It is ancient practices that serve people by keeping us in harmony and balance, both within ourselves and with each other. These ancient practices assist us to tap into the laws of nature and creation so we can flow with these natural currents of life without having to manage our lives on a purely physical or practical level. The practices and initiations awaken our own inner knowledge and expand our consciousness to see and know things in remarkably new ways.

This tradition has no institutional facilities, nor hierarchy of leaders who tell people how they must behave. Rather it is a tradition that works on the mystical and energetic levels. It understands we are part of a larger whole. The sun that rises everyday gives us life. The seeds we plant give us sustenance. It is a tradition that knows we reap that which we sow. It is a tradition that knows the importance of *ayni*, reciprocity – the principle that what we give, we receive and what we receive we give. This is the law of nature, the created order of things. It's about living in right relation with ourselves, others and all of creation.

The Andean tradition reminds us we are intimately connected with everything and everyone around us. If we are in balance, then we are in rhythm with the natural flow of things. Life then requires much less effort to accomplish so much more.

Yes, the Andean tradition has indigenous practices local mountain people have done for hundreds even thousands of years, working with plants, coca leaves and elements of nature. There are ceremonies, rites and rituals used to heal and assist members of the community. A key element to keeping these practices and teachings alive includes initiation rites (*karpays*, energy transmissions) that are passed from master to apprentice if someone in the community is called to leadership in the tradition.

This is the area around which much of the discussions about authenticity are focused. This tradition, up to recently, has been an oral tradition, passed down through initiation rites as well as an apprenticeship system where people learned the practices and rituals as part of their experience in the communities. Since many high altitude communities were not very easily reached, the Spanish had difficulty converting these indigenous practitioners to the Catholic religion. Many shamans who are alive today, who became Catholic over the years, still practice their ancient traditions, not as a religion but as a way of life. For them, there is no conflict.

All this is to say that like any evolving social, practical, spiritual system, many ways and varieties of practices exist harmoniously within this tradition. No one is more authentic than the other. They continue to thrive because they work.

There are many people who have learned these ancient practices from indigenous mountain shamans in Peru and shared the teachings with people around the world who resonated strongly with these practices because they touched something in their core. I first heard about this tradition when Alberto came to Johannesburg. He had been visiting Peru and studying with shamans there for more than 20 years at that point.

During my first trip to Peru six months later, I met several other people who were teaching the Andean tradition, including Regis and Sergio who became my teachers by responding to my request to teach a workshop in Johannesburg, where I was then living. I am extremely grateful to them for all they taught me. In addition to Alberto, Regis and Sergio, I have met other Peruvian teachers, well educated and professional, who learned the tradition from indigenous shamans – Juan Nunez Del Prado, Jose Luis Herrera, Oscar Miro Quesada, to name just a few. Then there are former students of these teachers who also teach.

They all have their own way of teaching the tradition. Thankfully there is no ultimate authority to say one is more "correct" than the other, although there are certainly people who have tried. Each of them has their own organization which orders how and when and where they pass on this tradition to others, both in Peru and around the world.

For example, I learned the method codified by Regis and Sergio. They called their organization The Order of Inkari. When it was time for me to leave their organization, I continued to teach many of the things they taught me – like the work with the four elements. I have also developed my own form and style of teaching I feel reflects the main principles of the tradition, even though it may differ somewhat from the things I learned from my teachers. For most teachers and students who become teachers, I imagine this is true and, in my opinion, as it should be.

I was reluctant at first to fully embrace the Munay-Ki Initiation Rites because I hadn't studied with Alberto and knew (as much as an outsider can know these things) that Alberto's way of teaching the tradition had different aspects from the way I had learned it. But after learning the Munay-Ki, and even more so after teaching it to others, I realized the energy of these Rites is profound and powerful. The form and substance of the Rites had been codified by Alberto but the energy and purpose of the Munay-Ki is connected to an ancient tradition that reminds us of who we really are, beyond culture and country.

Alberto offered the Munay-Ki outside of his own organization, setting it free to spread as far and wide as it has within only a few years. The world-wide interest in these rites is evidence they are awakening people to wisdom and knowledge held for many years by

215

only a few, mostly in remote areas. Some indigenous people in other parts of the world have guarded carefully their ancient teachings and practices. But the shamans in the Andes of Peru have welcomed the interest of Peruvians and foreigners alike. They believe the time has come to share these rites to assist humanity to manifest the new golden age of their prophecies. Alberto shared this belief which is why he allowed the Munay-Ki to spread without seeking to control it or profit from it. Everyone who teaches it is invited to do the same. There is no way to control the Munay-Ki because it is shared freely for people to benefit from it or not.

So the issue of authenticity for me becomes moot. This is the moment of history where all humans are invited to recognize our connection with one another. With each interchange both foreigner and indigenous become altered. We effect change in one another. This is the reality. When the Dalai Lama visited Cusco in 2005 he said it is important for his people in Tibet to preserve the essence of their ancient teachings but also to learn how to live in the modern world and benefit from the new technologies. How to navigate this mix of culture and tradition, antiquity and modernity is what we are all learning how to do, indigenous and foreign alike.

We live in a time when we each can learn from one another how to become our best selves. I choose to practice and teach the Andean tradition because it empowers me and the ones I teach it to. I delight in the fact the tradition has no fixed organization nor hierarchy of leaders, no dogma of beliefs and no one to tell you if you are bad or good. No one to kick you out if you don't do as the people in power say.

The time of hierarchy, ego-power and control is over. What is special for me about the Nine Munay-Ki Rites is that anyone who wants them can receive them. After learning how to give them, you can share them with as many people as you'd like and teach others how to do the same. People are drawn to them because they change lives in a positive way. People are free to participate or not, to grow the seeds or not. No ultimate authority is needed to control the movement of the rites. There exists the trust and belief that through these rites we are connecting to a higher source, to become co-creators of the world we are dreaming into being.

APPENDIX C – Archetypes of the Harmony Rite

Here are some descriptions of the archetypes you might find helpful in your work with them. In addition, recipients are invited to develop their own relationship with the archetypes, from their own experience.[7]

SERPENT This archetype is given into the first or root chakra. The Serpent is the Mother of the Waters and has been the archetype of the healer throughout many cultures. The staff of medicine, or caduceus, is formed by two serpents intertwined around a rod. The Serpent teaches us to shed our personal past the way she sheds her skin. This archetype is the primary life force, the one who dives deep inside and knows the way into the deepest places inside ourselves.

Serpent walks with beauty on the belly of the Mother and knows the way back to the Garden, the place of innocence. She symbolizes knowledge, sexuality and healing. Serpent represents the primeval connection to the feminine and thus is a symbol of fertility. She symbolizes the essential life force that seeks union and creation. We can summon the creative principle by calling on this archetype of Serpent.

There is an Andean legend that tells the story of two mythical beings, Yacumama and Sachamama, represented by two big snakes that leave the underworld and ascend to the world of the here and now. Yacumama slithers along the earth becoming a great river and Sachamama walks erect with the appearance of an aged tree. She has two heads, the upper one feeds on birds and the lower one attracts the animals living on the surface of the earth.

These two snakes, when moving to the upper world, transform Yacumama into the lightning and Sachamama into the rainbow.

---

7   Special thanks to Alberto Villoldo and my South African friend Heather Morgan for much of the information about the archetypes.

This symbolizes the fertility and productivity of humanity and the earth. The three worlds unite through these two serpents that represent the energy of water and fertility.

JAGUAR/PUMA This archetype is given into the second chakra (abdominal area). This archetype is the Mother-Sister Jaguar who knows the way across the rainbow bridge to the world of mystery. She is the one who swallows the dying sun, teaching us to step beyond fear, violence and death. The archetypal connection to the life force of the jungle, she is the steward of the life force, a Luminous Warrior who has no enemies in this world or the next. This archetype represents the Life/Death principle and renewal.

Jaguar/Puma helps us navigate the changes we go through on a regular basis. In order for something new to grow, we need to release the old, creating space for the new to unfold. This archetype teaches us how to be present with each moment of our process, knowing when to be still and when to move. The Jaguar/Puma is fully present, fully grounded and sure footed. She has a deep inner knowing and a sense of what her next step should be. She then proceeds with it fearlessly.

Where Serpent represents the power of healing, which is gradual and incremental; Jaguar stands for sudden transformation, fire and death. It might seem odd to us the transforming force in the Universe is also associated with death. That which endured was always changing and renewing itself; that which remained unchanging, perished. The Ancient Americans recognized chaos and order, expansion and contraction, as the natural cycle of life.

We can transform our bodies so they heal more rapidly and age more elegantly by embodying the forces represented by Jaguar/Puma. Like a cat with many lives, we need to release the old life in order to leap into the new one. Otherwise, we can spend years patching and fixing an old self we have outgrown.

The Puma represents courage, bravery, cunning, shrewdness, perseverance and clear judgment. Physically, she is agile and strong, able to jump off a tree in two steps and swim across a large river against the current!

This archetype is a magical, mythical feline connected to the darkness of the night. Her eyes shine in the night, representing 'the one who sees in the dark, who can see the invisible, unveiling what hides in the shadows'.

She brings us to a point where we face our own death, leaving all fears and worries behind. Working with this archetype we take a conscious leap from the material to the spiritual world. Puma connects us to the path beyond death, guiding us to walk with courage, bravery, daring and tenderness, all at the same time.

HUMMINGBIRD This archetype is given into the third chakra (belly). This archetype connects us with the Ancient Ones, the ancestors, Grandmothers and Grandfathers, ancient memories and ancient wisdom. Working with the Hummingbird, we can step outside of Time to remember the ancient ways.

The hummingbird is the smallest bird in the world, a beautiful, unique bird, with feathers in all the colors of the rainbow. It only weighs between 2 grams (the Bee Hummingbird) and 20 grams (the Royal Hummingbird). It has a long, narrow beak and a tongue shaped like a trumpet. Siwar Qenti, the Royal Hummingbird, lives between 2000 and 4000m above sea level and although it lives in a community, it is able to retain its independence. Thus it is individualistic and collective by nature, quite similar to humans.

The Hummingbird drinks directly from the nectar of life, feeding from many flowers, learning from nature. Interestingly, it is most attracted to red flowers, and red is the color of the spirit of life. We can emulate the hummingbird and "drink" from the teachings of many teachers, the environment and from life itself.

The Andean people recognize the hummingbird as the wise being who knows how to drink from Life's nectars in the most audacious and conscious way. From this quick, light and beautiful bird, we can learn to think fast and foresee the future in order to create the most appropriate surroundings for our evolution. Each day we can strive for a lighter and swifter flight to reach the highest realities which are also our deepest inner realities. The hummingbird teaches us to recognize the beauty in everything and use it to bring freedom to our existence.

Even though Hummingbird was not built for flight, it undertakes and accomplishes the impossible journey. It flies thousands of kilometers from Canada through Mexico and Brazil to reach Peru in its yearly migration. It never tires, stops or loses direction. This bird embodies perseverance and exudes a sense of adventure. The hummingbird has no need to doubt its strength or wonder where the next meal is coming from, because it doesn't stop to think and worry. It just follows its heart.

Hummingbird is driven by love and light, to drink the sweet nectar of life itself. It takes us to the language of the soul, carries us into the realm of dreams, of poetry, of the arts, of images, of beauty, of truth and wisdom. Then we are able to embark on our inner journey. It is from the space of the hummingbird that we can see our experiences as part of our own Sacred Journey into Being. Hummingbird teaches us to live life fully.

CONDOR/ EAGLE This archetype is transmitted into the fourth chakra (heart-center). It is the great archetype of the East, the place of the rising Sun, the place of our Becoming. It embodies the principle of seeing from a high perspective. It brings vision, clarity, and foresight. The great wings of the condor hold the heart and teach us to see with the eyes of the heart. The Condor/Eagle energy pushes us out of the nest to spread our own wings so we may always fly wing to wing with the Great Spirit.

Condor/Eagle perceives the entire panorama of life without becoming bogged down in its details. This archetypical energy helps us find the guiding vision of our lives. The eyes of the Condor see into the past and the future, helping us to know where we come from, and who we are becoming. Eagle allows us to rise above the mundane battles that occupy our lives and consume our energy and attention. They give us wings to soar above trivial day-to-day struggles into the high peaks close to Heaven. Condor/Eagle represents the self-transcending principle in nature.

The Eagle is a very beautiful and powerful bird. Eagle is strong with powerful claws and extremely sharp, clear vision, allowing him to see minute details from vast distances. Some eagles have two focal points in their eyes, one for frontal vision and one for lateral distant vision.

Condor, the largest bird on the planet, can have a wing-span of between 2.70 and 3.30 meters (between 9- 11 feet). It can fly at altitudes between 3,000 and 7,000 meters, where it glides for hundreds of kilometers with virtually no movement of its wings, thus expending very little energy. It has its habitat high in the Andes. In Incan times, the Condor was believed to be immortal.

The Condor symbolizes force, intelligence and exaltation. According to myth, when the Condor feels it has reached old age and its life force is running out, it settles on a high peak in the mountains, folds its wings, and picks up its feet, and plummets to the depths below, thus ending its reign. Then the Condor returns to its nesting place and is reborn into a new cycle of life.

This archetype assists us with clarity and discernment in our lives. These lend purpose and meaning to our existence, allowing us to live and see situations and people from a higher perspective.

KEEPER OF THE LOWER WORLD/HUASCAR This archetype is transmitted into the fifth chakra (throat). Historically, Huascar was one of two sons of the last Inka. He was the keeper of the medicine teachings and was killed by his brother, Atahualpa, who then banded together with the Spanish. This archetype is the harmonizing principle of the Lower World – the chaotic dark place of all creative potential.

Huascar, a frightening figure with a heart of gold, calls us to meet our fear and step out of our darkness into the light. He stands ready to assist us. The gift of Huascar is to harmonize our relationship with our Shadow.

There is a lake just outside Cusco called Huacarpay. A mythical story says the spirit of Huascar resides in that lake. The story says when he was killed, the Spanish cut off his limbs and put them in the four corners of the Empire to assure the Inka royal line would never rule again. His heart is in that lake, they say, and when the world is once again in harmony, he will rise from the waters to assist in the dawning of the new golden age of peace and unity.

KEEPER OF THE MIDDLE WORLD/QUETZAL-COATL This archetype is transmitted into the sixth chakra (third eye). This archetype from Mayan mythology is the Lord of the Dawn, the Day Bringer, the Morning Star. Quetzalcoatl brings harmony and order. Quetzal is a beautiful jungle bird and coatl is a serpent. A feathered, winged serpent that has acquired flight is the organizer of the material world. Quetzalcoatl is said to have brought irrigation, medicine plants and stonework to the Americas. He brought stability, music, dance, flutes and drums. Though this mystical creature has been lost in our culture, we can call on its animistic knowledge of the ways of the Earth to organize our relationship with the practical material world. When you come into relationship with Quetzalcoatl, you no longer have to micromanage your life.

The attributes of Quetzalcoatl are very similar to those of Manco Capac and Mama Ocllo in the Inka tradition. As children of the Sun, they were given the task of founding the Inca Empire. They were also mythical characters, said to rise out of the waters of Lake Titicaca. They were taught agricultural as well as all the necessary skills for life on this earth plane. Taytay Inti (Father Sun) then gave his children a golden rod and told them that wherever the rod sank with one thrust into ground as soft and fertile as the human navel would be the center of the Empire. The rod stood upright in Cusco, whose name means "navel" in Quechua. Manco Capac and Mama Ocllo won the local people over by teaching them a more advanced form of civilization.

PROTECTOR OF THE UPPER WORLD/PACHAKUTI This archetype is transmitted into the seventh chakra (crown). This archetype is connected with the time to come, the keeper of possibilities, the organizing principle of the Upper World. It embodies the concept of circular time, or stepping outside of linear time. This archetype can make time stand still, bringing heavenly order to Earth. By coming into relationship with Pachakuti, we recognize what can be changed and change it before it is born.

Pachakuti is the guardian of the gates to the Hanaq Pacha (upper world) and will accompany and support us in our journey through this realm. This is the realm where we experience everything in a space beyond linear time, the place of possibilities and creation. Here we can change our energy vibration and access more expanded aspects of our selves. Working with this archetype, we move beyond our physical body to experience ourselves as pure energy to meet the evolved person we are becoming.

GLOSSARY

ALTOMISAYOQ Traditional Andean shaman who works with the apus. The Altomisayoq initiation rite is the equivalent energy to the Wisdomkeeper Rite in the Munay-Ki

APU(S) Spirit of the mountain(s)

AYNI Reciprocity, exchange

CHAKANA Inka cross with four equal arms, three "steps" on each side and a hole in the middle. A sacred symbol in the Andean Tradition.

HUASCAR Historically, Huascar, one of two sons of the last Inka was killed by his brother, Atahualpa, who then banded together with the Spanish. In the Munay-Ki, Huascar is an archetype of the Harmony Rite, who is the harmonizing principle of the Lower World. (see Appendix C)

KURAQ AKULLEQ Literally it means the elder who chews coca, and refers to a high level shaman in the Andean Tradition with many years experience. The Kuraq Akulleq initiation rite is the equivalent energy to the Earthkeeper Rite in the Munay-Ki.

LLANKAY Work or service. This traditional principle of life is associated with the energetic doorway of the navel.

MAMA UNA Mother Water

MANCO CAPAC and MAMA OCLLO in the Inka tradition were mythical characters said to rise out of the waters of Lake Titicaca. As children of the Sun, they were given the task of founding the Inca Empire.

MESA Literally, mesa means table or altar. In the Andean Spiritual Tradition, a mesa contains sacred stones wrapped in a hand-woven cloth which is used by the shaman for healing and empowering.

MUNAY Love. This traditional principle of life is associated with the energetic doorway of the heart center.

MUNAY-KI I love you

NINA Fire

PACHAKUTI In the Munay-Ki, Pachakuti is an archetype of the Harmony Rite, connected with the time to come, the keeper of possibilities, the organizing principle of the Upper World. (see Appendix C)

PACHAMAMA Mother Earth

PAMPAMISAYOQ Traditional Andean shamans who work with Pachamama, using healing herbs and plants to assist their community. The Pampamisayoq initiation rite is the equivalent energy to the Daykeeper Rite in the Munay-Ki

PI STONE A donut shaped stone used to give the Munay-Ki Rites. The Pi Stone is symbolic of our luminous energy field. Its circular shape represents the archetype for wholeness.

Q'AWAC To see, to look; person who reads coca leaves and sees what they say

Q'ERO Person from a specific group of communities (Q'eros) high in the Andes of Peru

QUECHUA Indigenous language spoken by the people of the Andes

QUETZACOATL From Mayan mythology, a feathered, winged serpent that acquired flight. In the Munay-Ki, Quetzacoatl is an archetype of the Harmony Rite who organizes the material world. (see Appendix C)

SONKO Heart

TARIPAYPACHA The mythical new golden age spoken of in the Inka prophecies

WYRA Wind; spirit of the wind

YACHAY Wisdom. This traditional principle of life is associated with the energetic doorway of the third eye.

ACKNOWLEDGEMENTS

Writer, teacher, artist Wendy Crumpler saw where my manuscript needed help and gently guided me to improve the content and flow. Three of her original pieces added clarity and depth to the story. In addition, she brought her artist flair to the beautiful design and layout of both book and cover and then shepherded it all through production.

Thank you Wendy, my best friend and sweet soul sister. Thank you for your invaluable help with this book and for 35 years of friendship, which encourages and inspires me to be my best self.

Thank you to Susan Macfarlane, who appeared at Paz y Luz at just the right moment. She agreed to edit the manuscript but ended up sharing so much more than her wonderful editing skills. Thank you Susan, for your inspiration, enthusiastic support and delightful friendship.

Thank you Sharon Dunn, for your editorial advice and for being such a caring sister-in-law.

Thank you Kirpa Carolina Bookless for your generous offer to proof read the manuscript, for your time, your insights and advice.

Thank you Barry Haynes, gifted photographer and friend, for some of the photos on the cover.

Thank you Claudia Edwards, for giving me the Munay-Ki Rites for the first time in June 2007. Thank you Jamee Curtice, for your friendship and for giving our first Munay-Ki workshop here at Paz y Luz in October 2007 where I learned how to give and teach the rites.

Thank you to all the people who invited me to teach the Munay-Ki around the world and for welcoming me so graciously in your countries: Sylvia Wray in Bariloche; Johan Svanborg in Skinnskatteberg (Sweden); Anneke Coopman and Rita Schoonman in Brummen (Netherlands); Jonna-Maria Heedahl in Copenhagen;

Amey Horning and Marsa Truscott in Michigan; Irene Viglia Atton in Vetan (Italy); Edwina Griffin in Sydney; Hetty Driessen in Gold Coast (Australia); Valentina Scognamiglio in Rome; Pia Sofia Koren in Jutland (Denmark); Lilian Dijkema in Lofoten (Norway); Heather Morgan in Midrand (South Africa); Linda Fredrickson in Cape Town; Glenn Meyer and Cleone Cull in Port Elizabeth; Anahata Menon, Megha Kumar and Anindita Menon in Mumbai; Srdjan Stankovic in Belgrade (Serbia); Norma Urquiza in Queretaro (Mexico); Ruby T. Ong in Hong Kong; Li Yen Chim in Kuala Lumpur; Katharina Bless in Chiang Rai (Thailand).

Thank you to the generous spirit of everyone who shared their stories with me of Munay-Ki magic: Karen Nielsen, Amerissis Feliz, Carol Masters, Jacqueline Wigglesworth, Sylvia Wray, Brigitte Meuwissen, Mary Sky, Louisa Callery, Steen Clausen, Lilian Dijkema, Judi Muller, Daz Taylor, Jonna-Maria Heedahl, Silvia Pratten, Kathleen Ruel and Cheryl Jackson.

Thank you Alberto Villoldo, for codifying the Munay-Ki in 2007 and setting it free to spread its magic around the world.

And thank you Christer, for all your love and support – for the writing of this book and living life fully.

ABOUT THE AUTHOR

Diane Dunn is a healer and teacher of the Andean Spiritual tradition. She is originally from New York and after a career in theatre, she attended Union Theological Seminary. In the 1990s, she worked in South Africa just after the liberation of Nelson Mandela, developing an outreach program for homeless and unemployed people in downtown Johannesburg. In 2000, she moved to Peru where she built and runs Paz y Luz (Peace and Light) Guest, Healing and Conference Center in Cusco's Sacred Valley. Her first book, *Cusco: The Gateway to Inner Wisdom*, was published in 2006. By invitation, she teaches the Munay-Ki around the world as well as in Pisac where her center is located.

Feel free to write Diane at cuscodiane@hotmail.com or visit the Paz y Luz website www.pazyluzperu.com

CPSIA information can be obtained at www.ICGtesting.com
Printed in the USA
BVOW05s0108240615

405887BV00001BA/25/P